A Companion to Antonio Gramsci

Studies in Critical Social Sciences Book Series

Haymarket Books is proud to be working with Brill Academic Publishers (www.brill.nl) to republish the *Studies in Critical Social Sciences* book series in paperback editions. This peer-reviewed book series offers insights into our current reality by exploring the content and consequences of power relationships under capitalism, and by considering the spaces of opposition and resistance to these changes that have been defining our new age. Our full catalog of *SCSS* volumes can be viewed at https://www.haymarketbooks .org/series_collections/4-studies-in-critical-social-sciences.

A COMPANION TO ANTONIO GRAMSCI

Essays on History and Theories of History,
Politics and Historiography

EDITED BY
DAVIDE CADEDDU

Haymarket Books
Chicago, IL

First published in 2020 by Brill Academic Publishers, The Netherlands
© 2020 Koninklijke Brill NV, Leiden, The Netherlands

Published in paperback in 2021 by
Haymarket Books
P.O. Box 180165
Chicago, IL 60618
773-583-7884
www.haymarketbooks.org

ISBN: 978-1-64259-425-6

Distributed to the trade in the US through Consortium Book Sales and
Distribution (www.cbsd.com) and internationally through Ingram Publisher
Services International (www.ingramcontent.com).

This book was published with the generous support of Lannan Foundation and
Wallace Action Fund.

Special discounts are available for bulk purchases by organizations and
institutions. Please call 773-583-7884 or email info@haymarketbooks.org for more
information.

Cover design by Jamie Kerry and Ragina Johnson.

Printed in the United States.

10 9 8 7 6 5 4 3 2 1

Library of Congress Cataloging-in-Publication data is available.

Contents

PART 1
History

PART 2
Theories of History

PART 3
Communism

        Alberto Burgio

PART 4
Hegemony

9   Gramsci: Political Scientist   93
        Michele Prospero

10   The "Prison Notebooks": Hegemony and Civil Society   105
        Giuseppe Cospito

11   On the Productive Use of Hegemony (Laclau, Hall, Chatterjee)   114
        Michele Filippini

PART 5
Historiography

12   The Influence and Legacy of Antonio Gramsci in Twentieth-Century
     Italy   127
        Marzio Zanantoni

13   The International Historiography on Gramsci in the Twenty-First
     Century   146
        Davide Cadeddu

     Bibliographic Abbreviations   155
     Index   156

Preface

Over the course of the twentieth century, Antonio Gramsci became an author so often cited and so extensively studied at the international level that it now sometimes seems his cultural origins have been overlooked. Thanks to translations of his writings into English (and many other languages), Gramsci's thought has acquired a truly global audience and inspired scholars in different disciplinary areas by reaching beyond the original utterance in Italian. Almost daily, new research is being carried out: articles and books are published completely neglecting the scientific literature produced in the language that he himself spoke. This can be considered legitimate when Gramsci's thought is – more than anything else – an occasion and a stimulus with the aim of saying something other than what he himself affirmed, but the difficulty of accessing the primary sources of his political thought can sometimes produce an unintentional misunderstanding and conceptual inaccuracy. Reflecting on the relationship between scholarly studies in Italian and in other languages may perhaps lead us to speculate that while the first might be able to guarantee a greater philological precision and hermeneutic penetration, the second may demonstrate themselves to be more prone to developing the reformulation of Gramscian categories in the areas of sociology and anthropology besides those of historiography and politics.

On the occasion of the 80th anniversary of Gramsci's premature death, therefore, it was thought to organize a sort of intellectual account of the situation, including some of the most important Italian scholars of Gramsci's thought, and to arrange their musings around the relation between culture and politics, history and historiography. The results of this work forms a type of "companion" that is useful for a deep understanding of this author within an international dialogue which must express itself, nowadays, in English.

The volume is organized into five parts. In the first two essays – entitled *Gramsci: From Socialism to Communism* and *Antonio Gramsci: the Prison Years* –, under the general heading of "History", a concise and updated reconstruction of his biographical events is offered. The second part, dedicated to the "Theories of History", provides three different perspectives – summarized by the titles *The Crisis of European Civilization in the Thought of Antonio Gramsci*, *Notes on Gramsci's Theory of History* and *The Layers of History and Politics in Gramsci* – permitting an analysis of the ideas and theories of history which emerge from Gramsci's writings. In the third part, addressing the concept of "Communism" – with the essays *Gramsci and Marx: Notes and Reflections*, *Gramsci, the October Revolution and its "Translation" in the West* and *On the*

Transition to Communism –, as well as the fourth part, dedicated to the category of "hegemony" – with the articles *Gramsci: Political Scientist, The "Prison Notebooks": Hegemony and Civil Society* and *On the Productive Use of Hegemony* (*Laclau, Hall, Chatterjee*) –, the most explicitly political themes are considered. Finally, in the last part, dedicated to "Historiography" – with the essays *The Influence and Legacy of Antonio Gramsci in Twentieth-Century Italy* and *The International Historiography on Gramsci in the Twenty-First Century* –, the timelines of twentieth century historiography in Italy are traced and a picture is painted of the reasons for the development of the principal problems surrounding the international literary output on Gramsci.

The collection of these essays exposes a view of the complex relationship between Antonio Gramsci and the twentieth century, a century that for reasons analyzed here in various ways showed itself to be very generous in conceding so much importance to one man amongst many men. This fact cannot be taken for granted. Gramsci died in 1937, in a century that was densely full of events and personalities. It is not a given that the twentieth century would leave space for a man such as Gramsci: someone who was politically defeated, physically disabled, (according to some) betrayed and who was also certainly the expression of a particular tendency of a current of political thought – Communism – considered by most (even well before the end of the 1900s) to be tragically flawed, in concrete political experience and therefore also in its theoretical formulations. Gramsci expressed his thought, then, in a country – Italy –, that is not always at the center of international attention. Thinking about the relation between Gramsci and the twentieth century or Gramsci within the twentieth century, first of all means this: remembering how the remnants of his experience and his political thought have surpassed the date of his death, invading and permeating the Italian and international political culture for the full duration of the twentieth century. Making the point of Gramsci in the 1900s signifies underlining how this author, as markedly different than others, became a century's indisputable protagonist – both for the infinite interpretations that he elicited as well as for the uses and abuses of his thought and life story, with the purpose of quickly becoming one of most translated and cited Italian authors of all time together with such illustrious personalities as Dante Alighieri and Niccolò Machiavelli.

Considering this relationship between Gramsci and the twentieth century, today, in the first quarter of the twenty-first century, also signifies something more – clearly connecting with the international dimension acquired by this author. The temporal reference, the twentieth century, therefore, also emerges fully pregnant from the point of view of declaring its own primacy over the spatial dimension. Certainly, it is possible and it makes sense, for instance, to think about the relevance of Gramsci's influence on Brazilian culture or to re-construct the debate between historians and political theorists in France or, furthermore, to consider new sources emerging from some Russian archive. All this is possible and makes sense. Still, the true relevance of this discourse is revealed by the consideration that Antonio Gramsci is a global author. Like all things pertaining to thought, principles and ideas, he can only be limited to and contained by a historic view leaving aside geographical or geopolitical confines. Through the categories of "before" and "after", we can better pursue the goals of valuing and understanding an intense and fecund historiographi-cal dialogue that still leaves much to be said on Gramsci in the twenty-first century while also leaving room to write about an author who has risen to the position of an absolute classic of political thought.

Acknowledgements

I wish to thank Professor Daniela Saresella, who had the idea of organizing (and helped me to arrange) the conference devoted to Antonio Gramsci that elicited many of these reflections, and Professor Antonino De Francesco, director of the Department of Historical Studies at the University of Milan, which financially supported the English translation. I would like also to thank Professors Marco Cuzzi and Irene Piazzoni, who supported me during the above-mentioned conference that took place in Milan (Italy) on October 2017, and Doctor Elia Zaru, who copy-edited the texts.

Notes on Contributors

Alberto Burgio
is Full Professor of History of Philosophy at the University of Bologna. He is a member of the Scientific Committee for the Italian National Edition of Antonio Labriola's works and the Scientific Committee for the Italian Edition of Marx and Engels' Complete Works. He is also member of the CeRC – Centre for Governmentality and Disability Studies Robert Castel and of the Permanent Seminar of Political Philosophy "Penser la transformation" at the Université Paul-Valery – Montpellier 3. Since July 2011, he is a member of Accademia delle Scienze dell'Istituto di Bologna (Italy). He has dealt with history of political philosophy and philosophy of history, with studies on Rousseau, Kant, Hegel and Marx, racism, nationalism and Italian Marxism. On Gramsci, he published the monographs *Gramsci storico. Una lettura dei "Quaderni del carcere"* (Laterza, 2003), *Per Gramsci. Crisi e potenza del moderno* (DeriveApprodi, 2007) and *Gramsci. Il sistema in movimento* (DeriveApprodi, 2014).

Davide Cadeddu
is Associate Professor of History of Political Thought at the University of Milan and Coordinator of the Scientific Committee of "Globus et Locus" association. Executive Editor of *Glocalism: Journal of Culture, Politics and Innovation*, he is member of the editorial board of "Il pensiero politico", editor of the series *Biblioteca di cultura politica europea* (Rubbettino) and *Filologia e politica* (Giappichelli), and director of the "Permanent Seminar on the Classics of the Political Thought" at Giangiacomo Feltrinelli Foundation. He collaborates with the *HuffPost* (Italian edition). He has mainly studied the history of twentieth century political thought, with emphasis on the problems of the relationship between politics and culture. He edited writings of Leo Strauss, Julien Benda and Norberto Bobbio, and published the monographs *Luigi Einaudi tra libertà e autonomia* (FrancoAngeli, 2018), *Reimagining Democracy* (Springer, 2012), *Adriano Olivetti Politico* (Edizioni di Storia e Letteratura, 2010).

Giuseppe Cospito
is Assistant Professor of History of Philosophy at the University of Pavia and member of the Scientific Committee for the Italian National Edition of Antonio Gramsci's Writings. He is also member of the International Gramsci Society and of the Scientific Committee of the *Gramsciana: Rivista internazionale di studi su Antonio Gramsci*, the series *Per Gramsci* (Edizioni Unicopli), the Ghilarza Summer School and the Fondazione Casa Museo Antonio Gramsci.

He edited (with G. Francioni and F. Frosini) A. Gramsci, *Quaderni del carcere, vol. 2, tomo 1* (Istituto della Enciclopedia Italiana, 2017); *Gramsci tra filologia e storiografia. Scritti per Gianni Francioni* (Bibliopolis, 2010); (with G. Francioni) A. Gramsci, *Quaderni del carcere, vol. 1* (Istituto dell'Enciclopedia Italiana, 2007). He published the monographs *Introduzione a Gramsci* (Il Melangolo, 2015) and *Il ritmo del pensiero. Per una lettura diacronica dei "Quaderni del carcere" di Gramsci* (Bibliopolis, 2011); En. tr. *The Rhythm of Thought in Gramsci* (Brill, 2016).

Angelo d'Orsi

was Full Professor of History of Political Thought at the University of Turin and is member of the Scientific Committee for the Italian National Edition of both Antonio Gramsci's Writings and Antonio Labriola's Writings. He founded and is editor of *Gramsciana: Rivista internazionale di studi su Antonio Gramsci, Historia Magistra: Rivista di storia critica* and also BGR. *Bibliografia Gramsciana Ragionata*, composed of three volumes (published the first: 1922–1965, Viella, 2008). He founded "FestivalStoria" (Italy) and was president of the Scientific Committee of Fondazione Luigi Salvatorelli. He has dealt with the history of historiography, political ideas and intellectual groups. On Gramsci he published *Il nostro Gramsci. Antonio Gramsci a colloquio con i protagonisti della storia d'Italia* (Viella, 2013), *Inchiesta su Gramsci. Quaderni scomparsi, abiure, conversioni, tradimenti: leggende o verità* (Accademia University Press, 2014), *Gramsciana. Saggi su Antonio Gramsci* (Mucchi, 2015) and *Gramsci. Una nuova biografia* (Feltrinelli, 2018).

Michele Filippini

is Assistant Professor of History of Political Thought at the University of Bologna and coordinator of the digital library Gramsciproject.org. He has mainly studied the history of Marxism, the birth of sociology in the nineteenth and twentieth centuries as well as the forms of political legitimation and political power. He is member of the editorial board of *Scienza & Politica* and *Politics: Rivista di studi politici*. On Gramsci, he co-edited *Gramsci e la sociologia*, special issue of *Quaderni di Teoria Sociale* (Morlacchi, 2013) and published the monographs *Using Gramsci: A New Approach* (PlutoPress, 2016), *Una politica di massa. Antonio Gramsci e la rivoluzione della società* (Carocci, 2015) and *Gramsci globale. Guida pratica alle interpretazioni di Gramsci nel mondo* (Odoya, 2011). He is also the author of *Leaping Forward: Mario Tronti and the History of Political Workerism* (Jve-Crs, 2012) and co-editor of *Mario Tronti, Il demone della politica* (il Mulino, 2017).

Guido Liguori

is Associate Professor of History of Political Thought at the University of Calabria, President of the International Gramsci Society Italia and Senior Editor of *Critica Marxista*. On Gramsci, he organized, with F. Frosini, the IGS Seminar on the "Prison Notebooks" and edited (with G. Baratta) *Gramsci da un secolo all'altro* (Editori Riuniti, 1999); (with F. Frosini) *Le parole di Gramsci* (Carocci, 2004); (with C. Meta) *Gramsci. Guida alla lettura* (Unicopli, 2005); (with P. Voza) *Dizionario gramsciano 1926–1937* (Carocci, 2009); (with L. Durante) *Domande dal presente. Studi su Gramsci* (Carocci, 2012); *Gramsci e il populismo* (Unicopli, 2019); A. Gramsci, *Masse e partito. Antologia 1920–1926* (Editori Riuniti, 2017); A. Gramsci, *Come alla volontà piace. Scritti sulla Rivoluzione russa* (Castelvecchi, 2017); and he published *Sentieri gramsciani* (Carocci, 2006; En. tr. *Gramsci's Pathways* (Brill, 2015); and Br. tr.) and *Gramsci conteso. Interpretazioni, dibattiti e polemiche 1922–2012* (Editori Riuniti, 2012).

Marcello Montanari

was Full Professor of History of Political Thought at the University of Bari and is member of the advisory board of *Il pensiero politico*. He has dealt with the history of Marxism and Italian political thought, publishing articles on Althusser, Lenin, Vico, Croce and Gramsci. He edited A. Gramsci, *Pensare la democrazia. Antologia dai "Quaderni dal carcere"* (Einaudi, 1997), and published *La liberta e il tempo. Osservazioni sulla democrazia tra Marx e Gramsci* (Editori Riuniti, 1991); *Studi su Gramsci. Americanismo, Democrazia e Teoria della Storia nei "Quaderni del Carcere"* (Pensa, 2002); *Politica e Storia. Saggi su Vico, Croce e Gramsci* (Publierre, 2007) and *Il revisionismo di Gramsci. La filosofia della prassi tra Marx e Croce* (Biblion, 2016). His latest books are *Cultura e vita politica nell'Italia del Novecento* (Liberaria, 2012); *Studi su Vico* (Pensa, 2013); *Pinocchio e le altre favole* (Aracne, 2014); *La storia non finisce* (Aracne, 2015).

Vittorio Morfino

is Associate Professor of History of Philosophy at the University of Milano-Bicocca, where he coordinates the Specialization Course in Critical Thoery of Society. He is Directeur de recherche at the Collège international de philosohie. He is member of the editorial board of *Quaderni materialisti* and *Décalages: An Althusserian Journal*. He was visiting professor at the Universidade de São Paulo, Université Paris 1 Panthéon-Sorbonne, Université Bordeaux-Montaigne and l'Universidad Nacional de Cordoba. He edited (with P.D. Thomas) *The Government of Time: Theories of Plural Temporality in The Marxist Tradition* (Haymarket Books, 2018). His other works include *Il tempo e l'occasione. L'incontro*

Spinoza Machiavelli (Led, 2002; Fr. tr. 2012); *Incursioni spinoziste* (Mimesis, 2002); *Il tempo della moltitudine* (Manifestolibri, 2005; Fr. tr. 2010; Sp. tr. 2013), *Plural Temporality. Transindividuality and the Aleatory between Spinoza and Althusser* (Brill, 2014); and *Genealogia di un pregiudizio. L'immagine di Spinoza in Germania da Leibniz a Marx* (Olms, 2016).

Stefano Petrucciani

is Full Professor of Political Philosophy at the Sapienza University of Rome and President of the Italian Society of Political Philosophy. He is member of the editorial board of the journals *La Cultura, Parole Chiave, Critica Marxista*, and of the scientific committee of *Iride* and *Fenomenologia e Società*. He is Editor-in-Chief of *Politica e Società*, foreign correspondent of *Actuel Marx* and member of the scientific committee of Fondazione Gramsci. The main subject of his research was the critical theory of society of the Frankfurt School. Recent works edited include *Storia del marxismo* (Carocci, 2015) and *Il pensiero di Karl Marx* (Carocci, 2018). He is author of *Introduzione a Habermas* (Laterza, 2000), *Modelli di filosofia politica* (Einaudi, 2003), *Introduzione a Adorno* (Laterza, 2007), *Marx* (Carocci, 2009), *Democrazia* (Einaudi, 2014), *A lezione da Marx* (Manifestolibri, 2014), *A lezione da Adorno* (Manifestolibri, 2017), *Marx critique du libéralisme* (Mimesis, 2018).

Michele Prospero

is Full Professor of Political Philosophy at the Sapienza University of Rome, Executive Editor of *Democrazia e diritto* and member of the direction committee of the Centro per la riforma dello Stato (Centre for the Reform of the State). His main interests are the Italian institutional system and the left-wing political thought. On Gramsci, he edited A. Gramsci, *Il Sindacato* (Bordeaux, 2017) and authored *La scienza politica di Gramsci* (Bordeaux, 2017). His works include *Storia delle istituzioni in Italia* (Editori Riuniti, 1999), *La politica moderna* (Carocci, 2002), *Politica e società globale* (Laterza, 2004), *Alle origini del laico* (FrancoAngeli, 2006), *La costituzione tra populismo e leaderismo* (FrancoAngeli, 2007), *Filosofia del diritto di proprietà* (FrancoAngeli, 2009), *Hans Kelsen* (FrancoAngeli 2012), *Il partito politico* (Carocci, 2012), *Il libro nero della società civile* (Editori Riuniti, 2013), *Il nuovismo realizzato* (Bordeaux, 2015), *La ribellione conservatrice* (Edup, 2019).

Leonardo Rapone

is Full Professor of Contemporary History at the University of Tuscia and member of the scientific committee of the Italian National Edition of Antonio Gramsci's Writings. He is executive editor of *Studi Storici,* member of the Scientific Committee of Fondazione Gramsci and of the journal *Annali della*

Fondazione Gramsci. He has dealt with the European left political tradition in the twentieth century (socialist and social-democratic parties, Socialist International, communist parties), the Italian antifascism and European integration. On Gramsci, he edited A. Gramsci, *Scritti (1910–1926), vol. 2, 1917* (Istituto della Enciclopedia italiana, 2015) and authored *Cinque anni che paiono secoli. Antonio Gramsci dal socialismo al comunismo* (Carocci, 2011). He published also *Trotskij e il fascismo* (Laterza, 1978), *Da Turati a Nenni* (FrancoAngeli, 1992); *Antifascismo e società italiana 1926–1940* (Unicopli, 1999); *La socialdemocrazia europea tra le due guerre* (Carocci, 1999); *Storia dell'integrazione europea* (Carocci, 2015).

Giuseppe Vacca

is President of Fondazione Gramsci and President of the Scientific Committee of the Italian National Edition of Antonio Gramsci's Writings. He was Full Professor of History of Political Thought at the University of Bari. He dealt with the first editions of Gramsci's *Letters from Prison* and *Prison Notebooks* and published *Togliatti editore di Gramsci* (Carocci, 2005). On Gramsci, he published *Gramsci e Togliatti* (Editori Riuniti, 1991), *Appuntamenti con Gramsci* (Carocci, 1999), (with C. Daniele) *Gramsci a Roma, Togliatti a Mosca. Il carteggio del 1926* (Einaudi, 1999), *Vita e pensieri di Antonio Gramsci (1926–1937)* (Einaudi, 2012) and *Modernità alternative. Il Novecento di Antonio Gramsci* (Einaudi, 2017). His works include *Fra Italia ed Europa* (FrancoAngeli, 1991), *Pensare il mondo nuovo* (Edizioni San Paolo, 1994), *Per una nuova costituente* (Bompiani, 1996), *Vent'anni dopo. La Sinistra fra mutamenti e revisioni* (Einaudi, 1997), *Da un secolo all'altro* (Bompiani, 1998) and *Riformismo vecchio e nuovo* (Einaudi, 2001).

Marzio Zanantoni

is Editorial Coordinator of Unicopli Editions in Milan. He has dealt with some topics of philosophy and historiography in Italian culture during the nineteenth and twentieth century. He edited (with A. Vigorelli) *La filosofia italiana di fronte al fascismo* (Unicopli, 2000); A. Labriola, *Origine e natura delle passioni secondo l'"Etica" di Spinoza* (Ghibli, 2004), A. Labriola, *Del socialismo e altri scritti politici* (Unicopli, 2004); (with A. Vigorelli) *Gramsci oltre l'ideologia. Letture e interpretazioni (1960–2010)* (Unicopli, 2011), (with A. Vigorelli) F. Fergnani, *Antonio Gramsci. La filosofia della prassi nei "Quaderni del carcere"* (Unicopli, 2011) and (with S. Mancini and A. Vigorelli) E. Agazzi, *La filosofia di Piero Martinetti* (Unicopli, 2016); and authored *Anarchismo* (Bibliografica, 1996), *Gramsci e la storia della nazione italiana nei "Quaderni del carcere"*, in *Gramsci oltre l'ideologia* (Unicopli, 2011), *Albe Steiner. Cambiare il libro per cambiare il mondo* (Unicopli, 2013), *Positivismo* (Bibliografica, 2016).

PART 1

History

..

CHAPTER 1

Gramsci: From Socialism to Communism

Leonardo Rapone

To understand Gramsci's journey from socialism to communism requires focused attention on the years between 1913–14 and 1919: the defining years of the intellectual and political maturation of Gramsci's personality. We do not know exactly when the young student joined the Socialist Party, but it certainly was sometime between the end of 1913 and the beginning of 1914 and thus this is the starting point of the journey from socialism to communism. Already in 1919 we can say that Gramsci was in the gravitational field of international communism but he would reach the arrival point of his journey exactly in 1921: the year the Communist Party of Italy was founded.[1]

It is wise to specify that there is no archival documentation on this period: we can reconstruct it only using public documents and public proceedings made by Gramsci – mostly in the form of newspaper articles. To this we can add a few private letters. The only resource coming out of the archives are the drafts that were sometimes kept from the censored articles, which were not authorized for publication during the years of World War I.

At the beginning of this journey, Antonio Gramsci is a young student at the Faculty of Literature of the University of Turin,[2] and is passionate about glottology and linguistics: a disciplinary field that will continue to keep his attention.[3] His first public act dates back to October of 1914, when Benito Mussolini communicated a political stance that was distant from socialist neutralism, that is, from the position that rigorously refuted Italian participation in the Great War that characterized the politics of the Socialist Party, and for this had become the object of strong criticism from almost all the leaders of the Italian Socialist Party. On this occasion, Gramsci puts pen to paper for the first time to write about politics and publishes an article defending Mussolini from the criticism and accusations that were begin levied by his party's members.[4] In the eyes of a large part of the militant socialists in Turin, this first public act put Gramsci in a bad light and for several months he was isolated and marginalized

---

1   Cf. Rapone 2011 for this part of the political and intellectual biography of Gramsci.
2   Cf. d'Orsi 1999.
3   Cf. Carlucci 2013.
4   Cf. PPW: 3–7 (Gramsci 1914).

by the party. He resumed political activity only near the end of 1915, when he began to work as a journalist, having been hired (once again in Turin) by the editorial board of "Avanti!".[5] Here is the fundamental point – Gramsci became a militant politician in the guise of a journalist. In the early years, his political activism was exclusively expressed in his journalistic activity. Furthermore, the articles he wrote were articles that were mainly inspired by the reality of the daily life of Turin's citizens – the events and happenings of life in Turin. More weighty articles from the early years are rare, articles that address questions of a more general relevance. Still, even in articles inspired by daily life in Turin one can extract important elements that help to examine the inner workings of his mind. In fact, commenting on the citizens' doings – taking a cue from the small episodes of daily life – Gramsci develops a series of considerations that illuminate us as to the ideal premise of his socialism: his vision of the world and his concept of moral life in particular. In this first phase, what is the political profile that can be inferred from his interventions? These are the war years and his political position is, above all, against the war. Gramsci leads a tireless campaign through his articles against nationalist rhetoric, against the cultural miseries of war propaganda and against the demagogic artifices to which Italian interventionists resort in order to excite public opinion.

Nationalism and patriotism act against some of the fundamental premises of Gramsci's socialist vision. From the outset, Gramsci thought of socialism as the stimulus for humankind to exit from the constrained dimension of its more immediate experiences, in order to consider itself part of a more vast community. Thus, Gramsci's socialism is from the beginning positioned in opposition to any form of corporatism, be it in the form of a category, a village, a neighborhood or a region. Nationalism is also a form of corporatism, to which Gramsci opposes with a strong sense of belonging to humanity – each community belonging to all of all humanity. In the beginning, Gramsci's internationalism is strongly inspired by the sentiments of the universality of mankind and the rebuilding of humanity. Even when the internationalist projection of Gramsci later on assumed a stronger classist coloring, the theme that could be defined as the unity of the world – the unification of humanity – would remain on its horizon, witnessing a plurality of ideal reasons not reducible only to class solidarity. This, for Gramsci, motivated the need to supersede the nation-state as a structurally inadequate space both for the development of cultural life and civil progress and the development of the economic fundamentals of associated life.

---

5   Cf. Martinelli 1972, Righi 2014.

In second place, from Gramsci's journalistic interventions, intransigence emerges as a normative criterion of political action. Gramsci's socialism is an intransigent socialism even more than it is revolutionary. Intransigence is a constitutive aspect, the principal animator of Gramsci's socialism, seen by him as a way of being, a philosophy of life to which one can inspire to *even* in politics. History for Gramsci proceeds thorough the clash of contrary positions; this is the law of movement: action-reaction, thesis-antithesis – never synthesis. His intransigent vision of socialism assumes this outlook: socialism should tend coherently and determinately to its ultimate ends, without losing itself in detours or without imagining being able to increase its force through commingling and combining with other forces. Naturally, above everything, Gramsci's socialism bows to the anti-reformist and anti-Giolittian definition. The selective reformism of Giolitti, that gave privilege to only some parts of the country, breaks the worker-farmer unity: the unity of the Italian people that Gramsci saw perfectly hinged on the alliance between the workers of the North and the farmers of the South. His vision was very influenced, initially, by the analysis of Salvemini. Dialoguing and subordinating himself to Giolitti, reformist socialists cooperate with this project of fracturing and division: the decomposition of the unity of the Italian people.

A new chapter of the intellectual and political biography of Gramsci opens after the first half of 1917, not only under the pressure of the Russian events (I will not dwell on this because it will be the subject of another specific inquiry) but also because from that moment, Gramsci begins to consider from a new perspective the war – that is going to be longer then expected. What comes to the fore in Gramsci's thinking about the function of war is that it acts as a factor mobilizing the masses and as the motor of a regime crisis. Later, he will use an efficient expression to describe these transformations caused by war – both structural and psychological. Gramsci will say, "War has enlarged society".[6] Through the prolongation of war, through the hardships and suffering that it arouses, it awakens masses of men from a condition of social passivity – of folding into the individual and local dimension – and it makes them sensitive to what moves beyond the sphere of immediate perception. War projects them into the larger dimension of society. Society then grows because new multitudes enter into the space of sociability, exiting from a state of solitude and isolation and becoming active subjects of history – they insert themselves into history. The war is "Great" exactly because it makes society great. Therefore, war is no longer a factor of inertia, acquiescence and social passivity; but on

---

6   Gramsci 1918a.

the contrary it is an experience, which activates and mobilizes collective energies.

A fundamental piece of information: in August 1917 Turin was the theatre of the most vastly insurgent popular movement against the war that Europe had known in those years (besides Russia obviously).[7] A large part of the managerial framework of Turin's socialism was made subject to repressive measures, and Gramsci found himself for the first time pushed to the frontline and forced in some way to assume direct responsibility for the political direction. In particular, he becomes the *de facto* director of Turin's socialist newspaper "Il Grido del popolo". Having a newspaper at his disposal, he uses it to undertake the work of political education. We arrive at another formative aspect of Gramscian socialism: the relationship between socialism and culture. From Gramsci's point of view, the acquisition of culture is considered a determining factor of the political constitution of the subject and therefore of the development of a revolutionary subjectivity. "Social conscience", Gramsci observes, "was formed not under the brutal goad of physiological necessity, but as a result of intelligent reflection, at first by just a few people and later by a whole class".[8] Gramsci does not believe in the socialism of "calloused hands", that is, the socialism that gushes naturally from the exploitative experience lived by the working class, but considers necessary a connection with cultural stimuli and motives. The criticism of the present, the projection into a different future, must be based on a methodical exercise of thought. Socialist consciousness is not the immediate reflex of the working condition: the feeling is not enough to trigger the spark of socialism if the mediation of culture does not intervene. Gramsci viewed culture as the antidote to the possibility of an oligarchic degeneration of the political community and *in specie* of the mass political parties and of the Socialist Party, as insisted upon by the analysis of Robert Michels. The spreading of culture is insurance against the risk of the concentration of power inside the Socialist Party – or in the future of a socialist society – in the hands of a limited oligarchy.

It is interesting to note, however, that in the moment in which he takes on political leadership functions of the socialist section in Turin (August-September 1917), the first initiative considering the post-war period where Gramsci calls on the section to mobilize itself is an action against the return of the Italian government to protectionist political practices. In that moment, during the war, Gramsci thus proposes to mobilize the socialist organization in

---

7   Cf. Monticone 1972: 89–144, Spriano 1972: 416–431.
8   AGR: 57–58 (Gramsci 1916).

Turin in the struggle against customs protectionism.[9] This tells us two things: that in this moment, Gramsci was absolutely not yet thinking about the possibility in Italy of an extension of the revolutionary process that had just started in Russia – we are in the intermediate phase between the February Revolution and the October Revolution; and that principle of international liberty in trade had a place of utmost importance in the socialist vision of Gramsci. In his eyes, protectionism is an agent of war, for the commercial revelry that it triggers. Therefore, if peace is to be guaranteed once the carnage of world war is finished, striving against the raising of new trade barriers is needed. But above all, protectionism for Gramsci appears to be anti-historical behavior, contrary to the interest of capitalist development. For Gramsci, productive forces generated by the capitalist system do not adapt themselves to the frame of the nation-state and tend rather to interpenetrate, developing transnational bonds of solidarity. At this moment, what is already hinted at is that contradiction between the transnational dimension of the economic processes and the national organization of politics and institutions, which will be presented in the *Quaderni* as the principal factor of twentieth-century social and political convulsions. The war appears to Gramsci to be a distortion of the pure capitalistic mechanism, contrary to the needs of development of this system and its complex. This also means that Gramsci is very far from the idea of imperialism as a superior phase of capitalist development. At the same time, free trade for him has a strong anti-reformist valence because its opposite, protectionism, englobing sectors of the proletariat in the system of protected interest – is an encouragement to the collaboration between the classes.

Only at the beginning of 1919, almost two years later, the theme of the actuality of the revolution entered Gramsci's view. In this moment what began to dawn on him was the catastrophic vision of the post-war capitalist crisis of the Bolsheviks and of the newly born Third International, which envisaged the destruction of capitalism as the only alternative to Europe's regression towards barbarism. Gramsci is strongly influenced by these first theorizations on the general crisis of capitalism and was strengthened in the conviction of the revolution's maturity in the light of the spectacle showed in the countries just coming out of the defeat of war, in which the default of state structures coincided with the diffusion of revolutionary movements. Only those that he called "proletarian revolutions of 1919",[10] referring to Germany, Bavaria, Hungary, and to analogous movements in Austria, convinced him that it was a passage through

---

9   Cf. Gramsci 1917.
10   Gramsci 1919.

a historical phase and that revolution could actually become a political program for Western Europe.

Setting out the conclusion, I want to quickly consider the starting point –
socialism – and the arrival point – communism – of Gramsci's intellectual and
political journey, which I outlined. The theoretical basis on which Gramsci
founded his loyalty to socialism is a conception of history in which the propul-
sive function of mankind encamps itself – a concept of humankind as a conscious and strong-willed entity, a creator of history and at the same time produced by history itself. The starting point is the tenacious will of humankind.
Gramsci operated within the context of a cultural climate marked by the anti-
positivistic reaction, by the rehabilitation of the subjective and spiritual side of
human experience and was strongly involved in it. The social-economic environment, the material conditions of existence cannot determine the human
path without humankind's intervention: a decisive possession of the space
that offers itself to human initiative. In this phase, there were two targets for
Gramsci's criticism: on the one hand, transcendentalism and providentialism
in the catholic vision of the relationship between God and the world; on the
other hand, the positivization of socialism – the reduction of historical materialism to a deterministic conception of development and the claim that the
scientific nature of socialism consists of the representation of social processes
as natural processes, without regard for human initiative. We arrive at the
question of the influence that idealism had in the formation of Gramsci's
thought, how Gramsci explicitly recognized later in his *Quaderni del carcere*
("Prison Notebooks") and in the letters that he would write from prison,[11] ad-
mitting to being in 1917 substantially "rather a supporter of Croce", without,
however, making reference to, as per self-censorship, the influence of Gentile.
In Gramsci's vision, idealism had the merit of having redeemed humankind
from the mortgages – from the religious transcendentalism and positivistic determinism; and the language of idealism was the one through which Gramsci
initially expressed his anti-providential and anti-naturalistic conception of the
history. Here arises the question: and Marx? What place does Marx have in the
conceptual universe of early Gramsci? Marx is hardly ever quoted; Gramsci
clearly reveals a certain initial difficulty in fully putting the vision of humankind as builder of history in relation to Marx's doctrine. It's almost as if Gramsci could not fully satisfy, remaining on the perimeter of Marxism, the need to
see the will and conscience placed at the center of the process of transformation.

---

11   Cf. FSPN: 355 (Q 101, § 11: 1233), letter to Tania Schucht, August 17, 1931.

Here then, he uses the conceptual apparatus, and also the lexicon of idealism, in order to express the volitional and activistic content of his vision of socialism. It is on this background that one needs to view one of Gramsci's most notable articles, which he wrote after the Bolsheviks take power. The article bears the title *La rivoluzione contro "Il Capitale"* ("The Revolution Against 'Capital'") in "Avanti!", December 22, 1917: the Bolsheviks did justice to the theories of Marx, those that foresaw that socialism could only appear on the scene at the end of a succession of historical phases that included a compulsory passage through capitalism. Now, though, my impression is that, beyond the title (self-consciously paradoxical) this article signals the real beginning of Gramsci's Marxism: the Bolsheviks did not overturn Marx, they overturned the deterministic interpretation of Marx, the pretense of deducing a theory of necessary succession of historical phases from historical materialism. This is the real beginning of the relationship of Gramsci with Marx also for an immediately evident reason: the Bolsheviks declare themselves Marxists, and thus, in the moment in which Gramsci puts himself in solidarity with the Bolsheviks and fully recognizes their political determination, he cannot avoid asking himself about the problem of his relationship with Marx. Consequently, Gramsci progressively persuades himself of the possibility of a non-naturalistic definition of Marxism: a reading of Marxism that gives space to the function of human will. Gramsci will understand Marxism as a philosophy that already contains the principle of the determining function of the subject in the construction of reality. The core truth of idealism – this becomes the fixed point of Gramsci's vision – that is the function of human will, is fully present in Marx's theoretical system so there is no more need for spurious grafts in order to found the politics of socialism on the principle of creative power of man.

As for the initial profile of Gramsci's communism, one observes that, beyond the immediate solidarity with the revolutionary process in Russia, reflecting on the chains of events Gramsci persuaded himself that the "essential" fact of the Bolshevik Revolution is the construction of a new type of State;[12] therefore not only the overturning of the old ruling classes, but the construction of an "organized system of power",[13] radically different than the typical one found in the liberal society of West: the *Stato dei Consigli*. Gramsci's adherence to communism is characterized by a strong underlining of the function that the *Stato dei Consigli* assumes not only in Russia, but also later in the "Revolutions of 1919" that reiterate that aspect from the Russian example and

---

12   Cf. Gramsci 1919b.
13   Cf. Gramsci 1919c.

are also being articulated in council movements. At that time – in the first
months of 1919 – Gramsci arrived at the conviction that the construction of the
Stato dei Consigli could be an equalizing factor for the revolutionary processes
in all of Europe: hence the commitment that, entering the orbit of communism, he put into the realization in Italy of that organizational model, through
the development and conversion of "commissioni interne" (internal union
commissions) into factory councils.[14] It is necessary to add, though, that the
factory councils were conceived as a the cellular base of an institutional system that should be characterized, at the same time, by a strong capacity for
control and command, by "a strong socialist State, that halts as much before
dissolution and indiscipline, giving back a concrete form to the social body,
defending the revolution from external aggressions and internal rebellions"
(*Lo Stato e il socialismo*, "L'Ordine nuovo", June 28-July 5 1919). Gramsci's new
state is at the same time *Stato dei Consigli* and State of Authority and Command: a State in which base units express direct participation by the masses to
organization of social activities and a State that exercises a disciplining function inside of the social body – democracy of the workers and dictatorship of
the proletariat. To the latter, Gramsci assigns a double function. On one hand
it has a repressive function – keeping counterrevolutionary forces in check,
consenting to the new dominant class to complete the revolutionary transformation; on the other hand it has a liberating function, because underneath the
protection of the dictatorship a new organization of power was consolidating
"into which the dictatorship, having accomplished its mission, will be
dissolved".[15] Authoritarianism and the exercising of force are conceived therefore as *temporary* characteristics of the new state under construction that then
must dissolve into a new system of liberty and democracy. With the assump-
tion of the theme of dictatorship, on Gramsci's horizon enters the question of
the historical task of the minorities – of that "aristocracy of statesmen": how he
defines the Bolshevik leadership,[16] that through the exercising of state power,
interprets the will of the multitude and guides it to its maturity towards an
adequate awareness of their position and of their interests. It is from this moment that he began to consider the problem of building social consensus towards the revolutionary project and the problem of the relationship between
different social groups mobilized or mobilizable in support of this project. This

---

14   Cf. Spriano 1971, Salvadori [1973] 2007.
15   AGR: 50 (Gramsci 1918b).
16   Cf. Gramsci 1919c.

is the starting point of one of the principal strands of Gramsci's subsequent elaboration of political theory.

Bibliography

Gramsci's Works and Abbreviations

Gramsci, A. (1914), *Neutralità attiva ed operante*, in "Il Grido del popolo", October 31.

Gramsci, A. (1916), *Socialismo e cultura*, in "Il Grido del popolo", January 29.

Gramsci, A. (1917), *I socialisti per la libertà doganale*, in "Il Grido del popolo", October 20.

Gramsci, A. (1918a), *Anche a Torino*, in "Avanti!", December 5.

Gramsci, A. (1918b), *Utopia*, in "Avanti!", July 25.

Gramsci, A. (1919a), *Vita politica internazionale* [11], in "L'Ordine nuovo", May 15.

Gramsci, A. (1919b), *Rodolfo Mondolfo: "leninismo e marxismo"*, in "L'Ordine nuovo", May 15.

Gramsci, A. (1919c), *La taglia della storia*, in "L'Ordine nuovo", June 7.

AGR: Forgacs, D. (ed.) (2000), *The Gramsci Reader. Selected Writings 1916–1935* (New York: NYU Press).

FSPN: Boothman, D. (ed.) (1995), *Further Selections from the Prison Notebooks* (Minneapolis: Minnesota University Press).

PPW: Bellamy, R. (ed.) (1994), *Pre-Prison Writings* (Cambridge: Cambridge University Press).

Q: Gerratana, V. (ed.) (1975), *Quaderni del carcere* (Torino: Einaudi), 4 vols.

Other Works

Carlucci, A. (2013), *Gramsci and languages: unification, diversity, hegemony* (Boston, Leiden: Brill).

d'Orsi, A. (1999), *Lo studente che non divenne "dottore". Gramsci all'università di Torino*, in "Studi Storici", 1, pp. 39–75.

Martinelli, R. (1972), *Una polemica del 1921 e l'esordio di Gramsci sull'"Avanti!" torinese*, in "Critica marxista", 5, pp. 148–157.

Monticone, A. (1972), *Gli italiani in uniforme 1915–1918. Intellettuali, borghesi e disertori* (Bari: Laterza, 1972).

Rapone, L. (2011), *Cinque anni che paiono secoli. Antonio Gramsci dal socialismo al comunismo (1914–1919)* (Roma: Carocci).

Righi, M.L. (2014), *Gli esordi di Gramsci al "Grido del popolo" e all' "Avanti!" (1915–1916)*, in "Studi Storici", 3, pp. 727–758.

Salvadori, M.L. [1973] (2007), *Gramsci e il problema storico della democrazia* (Roma: Viella).

Spriano, P. (1971), *L'Ordine nuovo e i consigli di fabbrica* (Torino: Einaudi).

Spriano, P. (1972), *Storia di Torino operaia e socialista. Da De Amicis a Gramsci* (Torino: Einaudi).

CHAPTER 2

Antonio Gramsci: The Prison Years

Angelo d'Orsi

1 Some Chronological and Methodological Clarifications

Gramsci spent time in several prisons (Regina Coeli in Rome, San Vittore in Milan, Civitavecchia, Turi...) and in two clinics (Cusumano in Formia and Quisisana in Rome). The task of reconstructing this long phase of Gramsci's life entails following two lines of study: (*a*) retelling the events in such a way that the reconstruction serves to illuminate the psychology, choices and ideas developed by Gramsci; (*b*) concentrating on the ideas and putting into focus their course while seeking to grasp elements of continuity and/or discontinuity.

During the period between his arrest and his death, there were six years (between the spring of 1929 and the spring of 1935) of powerful theoretical creativity starting from the moment in which he was allowed to write for a few hours each day in his cell, keeping a limited quantity of necessary materials (notebooks and volumes) for this allotted number of hours.

From the moment of his arrest (November, 1926) until the beginning of the *Quaderni del carcere* ("Prison Notebooks") (February 1929), Gramsci did not remain inert: first of all, there are his letters and then there is evidence of study that bears witness to the pedagogical-political work he developed during his confinement in Ustica. With regard to the letters, it is immediately necessary to specify (for me it is a reconfirmation) that they should not be understood as private, emotional or affective, that is, the representation of Gramsci the man – the medium through which he confided his hopes and pains, his illusions and delusions – but as a body of work that can be considered along with the *Quaderni del carcere* ("Prison Notebooks"), providing important clues for their understanding. The *Lettere dal carcere* ("Letters from Prison") help us not only to correctly place the texts enclosed within the 33 Notebooks on the temporal plane, but also to understand them. One must underline the fact that Gramsci's letters are stuffed (almost to the point of redundancy) with bibliographic notes, linguistic, philosophical, literary, theatrical, artistic and historical ideas as well as historiographical indications. This implies the need for a parallel reading of the two bodies of work, or even a blended reading that integrates the letters with the notebooks and vice versa.

It is worthwhile to briefly summarize Antonio Gramsci's life path after his freedom was taken from him. The "prison years" need to be factually unpacked. The expression "prison years", at the same time both too wide-ranging and too generic, is made up of at least four phases in which different situations are determined:

a)   first, the 15 days spent in Regina Coeli prison: the traumatic moment immediately after his arrest. As Gramsci defined it: "the worst of my detention".[1]

b)   Then, a sudden and unexpected forced trip to the island of Ustica following a conviction with police internment. There is a certain amount of literature on this experience (testimonials, letters and even some films) that needs to be investigated in depth for its future educational implications not only from the political but also from the social point of view in relation to both his fellow inmates as well as the island population.

c)   Then, the long period of incarceration in San Vittore from January 1927 to May 1928 that in turn has become a recent object of investigation, but with very conflicting results.

d)   Subsequently, after a short time in Regina Coeli, the destination of the "maxi trial" was looming for the convict in Turi – the prison par excellence. Today, we have more knowledge about this time. The five years spent at Turi, however, should be analyzed diachronically, considering the whole period of time, since during the imprisonment there was a worsening of the rules that regulated the inmate's life and also because Gramsci's health conditions were progressively deteriorating.

e)   After a couple of weeks at the infirmary of the Civitavecchia prison Gramsci continued his recovery at the Cusumano clinic in Formia (November 1933). Initial high hopes were soon lost: while Gramsci was at the clinic with its semi-detention conditions, he did not receive the medical assistance that he and his family had had hoped for.

f)   Finally, Gramsci was returned to Rome (August 1935), this time at the Quisisana clinic, with a modest improvement in living conditions. This, however, was not enough to enable the full recovery of the patient.

These scans are necessary in order to more precisely position the thoughts that Gramsci entrusted to his notebooks. Still, philology and chronology must not take the upper hand as it could lead to a shattering of the *Quaderni del carcere* ("Prison Notebooks"). Even in their improvised and fragmentary form, the *Quaderni del carcere* still constitute "a work" in a certain way. The same necessary attention paid to the timeline – not only should stop us in front of the

---

1   Gramsci 1994a: 45, Gramsci to Tatiana, December 19th, 1926 (LC: 17; LT: 13; LC2: 14).

impossibility, no matter how many efforts are made, of dating every single note of the 33 Notebooks – and should oblige us also to notice that in Gramsci's process emerges a desire to overcome or at least to limit the fragmentary nature of the works (even though the thoughts are written in a dialogue format). Thus, in a certain sense, the work is "fragmentary". Otherwise, why at a certain point did he feel the need to rewrite, to return to texts already written and even to sketch essays (in the "special notebooks")? In short, what is evident is his will to go beyond the fragment and to give, with the passing of months and years, a more systematic and organized character to his own reflection.

There is a nexus between the logistical situation (the physical and psychological condition) of the prisoner and his intellectual work. A serious parallelism can be established between the degradation of the physical (the sickening body) and theoretical elaboration, reflection and self-reflection, on his personal, private, emotional affairs; even the writer's style is affected and this should be subject to a more reasoned assessment. In general, however, the elaboration of Gramsci's thought is very strongly conditioned by the concrete situation in which he finds himself living: the constriction, both physical and mental, that he is subjected to by force; the acknowledgment of the blocked political situation and the observation of the historical course that does not adhere to the vision held before his loss of freedom. Above all, the perception of defeat – the central idea, the common thread of Gramsci's thinking and feeling after November 8th, 1926 – is the fundamental evidence that the course of time led to a rethinking of his own theories: a dialectic between continuity and discontinuity which must be followed with maximum attention. Another dialectic, this time human, must also be taken into account. Between serenity and prostration, between the desire to fight and the desire to abandon oneself, "like a pebble in the current". On November 20th, a few days after his arrest, he wrote to his mother:

> I am tranquil and serene. Morally I was prepared for everything. Physically too I will try to overcome the difficulties that may await me and to keep my balance. You know my character and you know that at the bottom of it there is always a quantum of cheerful humor: this will help me live.[2]

That bit of humor, over the years, before the elimination of every possibility of returning to freedom, would lessen into a gradually more tired dialectic, between the "principle of hope" and the "principle of desperation".

---

2 Gramsci 1994a: 37, Gramsci to his mother, November 20th, 1926, (LC: 7; LC2: 6).

2   From Regina Coeli to San Vittore

A clear reconstruction of every detail of Gramsci's arrest is, to date, almost impossible, as is the dismissed hypothesis of a conspiracy within the Party to lure its leader into the fascist trap. We know that the quarrel amongst scholars is still ongoing (and not without bitterness) on the subsequent events after the brief interlude at Ustica when Gramsci, leaving behind the anguishing discovery of prison life in its most crude and brutal aspects at Regina Coeli, found a form of freedom for a month and half. Freedom from dawn to dusk, in the small enclosure of the island with strong limitation placed on his contact with the islanders, but it was still the immense joy of being able to enjoy the open air, seasoned with an even greater kind of pleasure: finding himself among comrades, not only communists, but also socialists, and other militants of the proletarian and anti-fascist movements. In Ustica, above all in tandem with Amadeo Bordiga (the fellow-adversary inside the Communist Party) with whom he shared his accommodation, Gramsci could apply his pedagogical inclinations, both with the "courses" he started in two disciplines (humanities and sciences), and with the basic work done together with his prison companions who were in need of literacy.[3]

In those 44 days he changed his legal status: from confined inmate he became a defendant in a series of serious crimes, for which a preliminary investigation and a criminal proceeding were planned. He had reached Milan, in "ordinary translation", where he was confined to the prison of San Vittore. The long and arduous journey from Ustica to Milan (19 days), was described by Gramsci in a famous letter, in which as well as showing his skill in writing narrative, he demonstrates a noteworthy capacity for anthropologic observation, but reveals also, almost flauntingly, his own capacity for endurance which at the time (January 1927) was still robust. Telling his sister-in-law Tania about that traumatizing experience, he was able to talk about it with the calm irony of a wise old sage:

> In general, the trip has been for me a very long cinematic event: I've come to know and I've seen an infinity of types, from the most vulgar and repugnant to the oddest replete with interesting traits. I've understood how difficult is to know the true nature of men from outward signs.[4]

---

3 There are no specific studies on Gramsci's stay in Ustica. Cf. the two interviews of islanders (Stochino 2016) and a recent film documentary titled *Gramsci 44*, by Emiliano Barbucci (2016).

4 Gramsci 1994a: 70, Gramsci to Tatiana and Giulia, February 12, 1927 (LT: 44)

He remained at San Vittore for almost a year and a half, a period during which the judge, Enrico Macis was able, with subtle cunning, to make the accused into a sort of victim-accomplice: to render him, to a certain extent, to be a collaborator in his own ruin.[5] Macis' lies did not only serve to worsen Gramsci's legal position, but also caused doubts and suspicions to grow in his mind, especially towards the Party, even though he was still leader. With the passing of the years and the worsening of his physical and mental health, these doubts and suspicions, would not have only not disappeared but would have flourished, because of a syndrome provoked by the sensation of affective solitude, isolation from the world and his tormented relationship with Giulia. Gramsci died without having found out about the truth about his arrest, the failed negotiations for his release, and the heavy sentence that weighed him down until the end of his life.

The case revolved around a letter that another important leader, Ruggero Grieco, had addressed to Gramsci, but also, some nearly exact copies sent to two other detained companions: Terracini and Scoccimarro.[6] Rivers of ink have been spilled on the subject of these letters, by the pressure of political and journalistic controversy more than the desire for an accurate interpretation – *sine ira et studio*.[7] Even if the hypothesis that it was a fake case constructed *ad hoc* by the police is true – excluding the idea that Grieco was a spy of the regime (excluding the fact that he wanted to harm his imprisoned partner) – what remains is only to interpret it as a gesture of thoughtlessness with the possible consequences not having being well calculated. Grieco probably had aimed to probe the capacity of repressive apparatuses while still showing affection and closeness to Gramsci and to the other two captive leaders. It was the judge who imprinted an unwanted meaning on that letter and it actually did not have that meaning in trial (according to the fact that the document was not used in the court arguments). Falling into Macis' trap, that letter became a torment for Gramsci that accompanied him to his death, in the fear of having been abandoned, if not betrayed by his Party outright, or at least by someone who made sure that he remained in prison. This someone, in Gramsci's mind, could have only been Togliatti, after the bitter exchange in the letter of October 1926 (regarding the struggle within the Russian Communist Party) and the consequent rupture of relations between the two. In reality, thanks to the special role of Piero Sraffa, the link between Gramsci and the Party, including

---

5   Cf. Giacomini 2017, conflicting with the interpretation of Fabre 2015.
6   Other than Giacomini 2017 cf. also Vacca 2012; d'Orsi 2018.
7   For the controversy surrounding the letter and other inherent questions on the arrest and imprisonment of Gramsci, refer to the d'Orsi 2014.

Togliatti, did not ever completely break, even if it sometimes unravelled to the point of rupture.

At the San Vittore prison, Gramsci carried the burden of several accusations that slowly worsened into a situation where he started to suffer abandonment – by the Party, even after failed attempts for his liberation, and from Giulia – revealing his own weakness, and at the same time, his own strength. The dialectic between these strengths and weaknesses would be the common thread of Gramsci's detention.

Not yet being a condemned inmate, but an inmate waiting for judgement, Gramsci had the possibility to write even to people outside of his family circle. The letter to Giuseppe Berti, his communist comrade, in which after having declared that he could not work and that his condition was not "worse than it was in the past years" and feigning tranquility: "I read a lot, but in a disorderly way", he added: "I possess a fairly happy capacity to find some interesting side even in the most modest intellectual production, such as serial novels, for example". We are at the beginning of the theory, later put into focus, of the "national-popular". In the same letter, he undertook a fast and efficient review of Nello Rosselli's book, *Mazzini e Bakunin,* proffering opinions of great interest. As a political leader, he gave method lessons to young historians: "I do not know Rosselli personally, but I would like to tell him that I do not understand the acrid bitterness he puts in his book of history". And then Gramsci descends into the details of his analysis, arriving at the conclusion that with an apology of "historical criticism", and an invitation to liberate oneself from certain diatribes of the past, perhaps even led by a mistaken point of view such as the one Rosselli ends up adhering to: namely a use of Mazzini against Garibaldi..., but generously acknowledging that the book "really fills a gap".[8] In this first period he still did not renounce his role as a studious professor even when he fully felt like a militant politician.

At San Vittore prison, Gramsci started to toughen himself, adopting rules for survival: "If one wishes to remain strong and keep intact one's power of resistance one must subject oneself to a regime and follow it with an iron will".[9] He found the force to tidy his cell, transforming it a small way into his "home". He gardened, planting seedlings, he raised animals such as sparrows, and he became an attentive observer of their habits.[10] At the same time, he made use of the prison's library and bought newspapers and weekly magazines at the

---

8   Gramsci 1994a: 128, Gramsci to G. Berti, August 8, 1927 (LC2: 103).
9   Gramsci 1994a: 137, Gramsci to Tatiana, September 12, 1927 (LC: 122; LC2: 115; LT: 135).
10   Cf. Gramsci 1994a: 125–126, Gramsci to Tatiana, August 8, 1927 (LC: 108–110; LC2: 100–102; LT: 125–127).

in-house reseller. He wanted to be involved the outside world, despite having been relegated to its margins, and intended to follow the events of men, books and countries.

Not having received permission to use paper and pen in his cell (except for his two weekly letters) Gramsci resorted to the strategy (that he must have thought up at the Turi prison) of inserting short book reviews, sketches of authors, and references to historical and philosophical analyses into his personal letters. Tatiana was the privileged recipient of these letters, who even with her limitations, tried at least to be an attentive listener, not possessing the ability to be a real interlocutor. The letters were a sort of anticipation of the *Quaderni del carcere* ("Prison Notebooks"). In one letter, the prisoner made an account of his typical day, punctuated by the prison timetable: besides the obligatory morning stroll and meals, his time was spent reading, studying, meditating, especially when at seven-thirty in the evening, the prisoners were forced to go to their beds. This was the moment when Antonio reflected on his day, on the time spent in prison, on his future prospects, on his wife Giulia and his children and, most likely, on the political situation.

Waiting to finally write in his cell, he made work programs, which corresponded on the one hand to an existential need, on the other to an intellectual need:

> I am obsessed [...] by this idea: that I should do something *für ewig* [...]. In short, in keeping with a preestablished program, I would like to concentrate intensely and systematically on some subject that would absorb and provide a center to my inner life. Up until now I've thought of four subject [...] and they are: (1) a study of the formation of the public spirit in Italy during the past century [...]. (2) A study of comparative linguistics! Nothing less; but what could be more "disinterested" and *für ewig* than this? [...] (3) A study of Pirandello's theatre and of the transformation of Italian theatrical taste that Pirandello represented and helped to form. [...] (4) An essay on the serial novel and popular taste in literature.[11]

This first program contained, in a nutshell, a part of the drama of the *Quaderni del carcere* ("Prison Notebooks"). The "für ewig", besides its translation ("forever" or "disinterestedly", such as was specified in another letter),[12] should not be

---

11   Gramsci 1994a: 83–84, Gramsci to Tatiana, March 19, 1927 (LC: 60–66; LC2: 54–58; LT: 60–63).

12   Gramsci 1994b: 155–157, Gramsci to Giulia, March 28, 1932 (LC: 597–599; LC2: 552–554).

understood as a disengagement, but rather as a departure from the immediacy
of the struggle with politics, overcoming the journalistic polemic and a reposi-
tioning in (not succumbing to) study. Gramsci took note of the situation in
which he found himself, and with the *für ewig* he seemed to announce the will
to resort to his own moral qualities, reasoning and writing with a spirt that was
"separated from contingent reality and from the political phenomena in
action".[13] The concept also seemed to indicated a double-sided will; the *resil-
ience in the prison*, more that the *resistance to the prison*; the determination to
go beyond the suffering, concentrating on his efforts, even in the absence of
interlocutors (that which he declared he always needed), without renouncing
the dimension of dialogue, that is the very form of Gramscian thought.

3   The Notebooks and the Letters: from Turi to Formia

Dubbed the "big trial", with a conviction of more than twenty years, arriving at
Turi Gramsci is now an inmate with a definitive sentence, needing to strength-
en his determination in order to keep working and to survive: something that
was granted to him only in February of 1929. The already severe prison rules
became even more rigid with time, in a paradoxical parallelism with the worsening state of the Gramsci's health.

In such an uncomfortable situation, Tatiana's proximity was providential
even if the pressures of his sister-in-law were often excessive and even wrong,
provoking contrariness in Antonio. The conclusion was always the same: who
is outside cannot understand what it means to be in prison. Giulia, his wife,
seemed to understand this least of all. Tatiana, on her part, does not only appear as an Antigone fighting against the tyrannical power that is killing Antonio (she is not only the one who tries to give him the strength to go on, but she
is also a woman in love) and in a certain sense, reciprocated by the man who
continues to reject the attitudes of those who are trying to give him comfort:
"I am not an afflicted person who must be consoled; I shall never become
one".[14] The man who continues to say that he has become insensitive: "in two
years", he wrote in October 1928, "I have lost almost all of my sensitivity" and
"the conviction of not being understood, to the limits within I am obliged to
write, pushes me lower and lower into a state of passive and blissful indiffer-
ence, from which I can not get away". A bitter paradox for one who a decade

---

13   Suppa 2016: 99.
14   Gramsci 1994a: 103–107, Gramsci to Tatiana, April 25, 1927 (LC: 82–85; LC2: 77–81; LT:
      95–99).

before shouted his hatred of indifferent people. The conclusion was dramatic: "I feel that I am sinking deeper and deeper".[15]

In spite of this, he started work in February – first with translation exercises (having important implications for content) introducing us to the grandiose construction of the *Quaderni del carcere* ("Prison Notebooks"). Laid out roughly following the plan enunciated in 1927, then re-worked two years later,[16] but enlarged according to different guidelines, between theatrical and literary criticism, history and historiography, philosophy and political science, economics and human and social sciences. A type of construction site that initially appears, for what one can reconstruct chronologically, really *in progress*, passing from more impromptu and provisional notes to an attempt at organic organization, within possible limits given the situation (lack of sources, censorship, constant aggravation of his health, progressive psychological prostration...). The letters are a snapshot of all this, but they are also a valuable tool for entering Gramsci's workshop and better understanding the innumerable implications.

In addition to the translation exercises, the drafting of the first notes of the *Prison Notebooks*, between 1929 and 1931 coincide with the "turning point" in the Comintern: the expulsion of Gramsci's friend Tasca by the Italian Communist Party and the expulsion of Trotsky from the Soviet Party – a moment of serious crisis within the international communist movement. It was an opportunity for Gramsci to rethink history and the problems of the community he feels a part of, with the distance of no longer being a political actor. He continues to think politically, even when the method is historical, and the disciplines that he practices are more varied. The *Prison Notebooks* propose a progressive emergence of concepts that Gramsci extracts, like Machiavelli (not by chance one his favorite authors) both from direct experience and from study. A work strongly steeped in history, in truth it transcends history and proposes an extraordinary repertoire of ideas in the working out of its themes. Hence the importance of dating, but without yielding philological exasperation (a very strong risk today in Gramscian studies), the different notes from the *Prison Notebooks*, taking into account that they have a sort of "reticular structure" in which the author proceeds with "spiral writing". Gramsci seems to want to put order, changing topic and at the same time changing notebook. This confirms the difference between the "miscellaneous" notebooks and the "special" notebooks, that is, monographic, in which there is a strategy of content characterization at the start of a new notebook. It is necessary to

---

15   Gramsci 1994a: 228–230, Gramsci to Tatiana, October 20, 1928 (LC2: 217–219; LT: 269–271).

16   Cf. Gramsci 1994a: 252, Gramsci to Giulia, March 11, 1929 (LC: 262; LC2: 244).

recognize Gramsci's rules. With that in mind one can try to enter the laboratory of the 33 *Quaderni del carcere* ("Prison Notebooks"), giving priority not to the mere chronology, but to the choice to reconstruct the lattice of themes brought into focus by Gramsci, who proceeds by reviewing the texts of the first draft (the "miscellaneous notebooks"), then adding and specifying and sometimes introducing changes into his work.[17]

Fragmentation of the draft (partly unavoidable, partly determined by choice, and thus the reference to "fragmentism", which corresponds to the dialogic will of the author) and, often, allusive writing (for fear of censorship and subject to self-censorship), do not prevent a result that, in the serious limits of the given situation, can be permissibly considered "a work". And despite the *für ewig*, the fundamental intent of the *Prison Notebooks* is political: a painful meditation on the defeat of the Party, the international movement to which it belongs, and on personal defeat – both as a manager and as a militant. To this is added the growing feeling of being vanquished as a man, husband and father: "understanding the reasons for the defeat was for him [...] the only way to continue the work of the revolution"; not just because he could not have done anything else while being in jail, but also because "from Marx he had learned that this is the only attitude of the revolutionary who does not resign himself to the subordinate part of the martyr". The militiaman had to become a man of science, without losing his militant spirit or renouncing the ultimate goal: the liberation of the oppressed classes.[18] We come across the term "defeat" 44 times in the *Prison Notebooks*, referring to historical situations, political events and the events of individuals. As he said several times, he was prepared for the eventuality: "since defeat in the struggle must always be envisaged, the preparation of one's own successors is as important is as what one does for victory".[19]

Some pages are obviously more political, even in encrypted form; others are a mediated discussion that favors a historical approach while also being attentive to the languages of the humanities and social sciences. The notes dedicated to the history of Italy are substantiated by politics, in which there is a constant cross-reference between past and present. Gramsci searches for the causes of defeat, but that means reflecting on the victors, *i.e.* the forces (Fascism) that beat the international proletarian movement, but also Americanism: in essence, the two faces of capitalism. Gramsci has an incredible ability to penetrate that world with analysis that, for many, seems to anticipate the analysis of the exponents of the "Frankfurt School". In relation to the crisis of

---

17   Cf. Francioni 2009, 1984.

18   Gerratana 1997: 55.

19   SPN: 153 (Q 14, § 70: 1734).

1929, a Gramscian reading challenges the stolid certainties of the Comintern and reverses the interpretation that sees the advent of communism within reach – with the certain and imminent collapse of capitalism. In any case, Gramsci sees a necessary phase of transition with the recovery of democracy. This is the meaning of the proposal of the "Costituente": a group of anti-fascist forces with a common orientation – a proposal which, in that historical-political climate, aroused strong opposition within the Party, creating difficulties for Gramsci in his relations with his prison companions. It was not a question of abandoning the socialist perspective or renouncing the option for radical change: Gramsci draws a different profile of the revolution, using the East-West ("Oriente"/"Occidente") opposition as a comparison, categories that are not merely geographical but economic, social, ideological and political. In the West, the revolution can no longer correspond to the Bolshevik model: the frontal assault on the Tsar's Palace. More than an act, it must be built as a process to replace the bourgeois hegemony and domination with that of the proletariat, working essentially in the fields of culture, thanks to the "organic" intellectuals of the working class, the exploited class and the oppressed: a class that can become dominant only if it is able to be hegemonic. Hence the importance of having one's own intellectuals, whose task is precisely that of helping the working class attain hegemony. Over time, Gramsci was beginning to see the transformation of this class, while he started talking about "subalterns" instead of "proletarians" or "working class": one of the great innovations of his intellectual work in prison, – alongside the concept of hegemony – seems to be among the main explanations of today's wealth of Gramscian thought, more adequate than that of other great thinkers of the transformation of the social and cultural characteristics of our time. But in the Gramscian reservoir, between 1929 and 1935, with a massive historical reconstruction, and a punctual, although not always consistent theoretical treatment, came to be set down a whole series of strong concepts: from passive revolution to hegemony, from national-popular to subaltern groups, from historical bloc to Caesarism, and so on – a reservoir on which today many disciplines draw on. Philosophy, historiography, sociology, anthropology, political science, literary and theatrical criticism, pedagogy and several social sciences are the varied landscape in which the work of Gramsci is located. From Turi to Formia, meanwhile, however, the inexorable degradation of his physical condition as well as his mental state took its toll.

The transfer to Formia, in the first of the two clinics that admitted Gramsci, his condition was in some ways even worse than when he was in prison. Having obtained semi-detention, in the establishment directed by Dr. Cusumano, he was subjected to even more intense police control than in prison.

In theory, he could receive whom he wanted, had the possibility of going out, moving away from the hospital perimeter, but the invasive police control combined with his constantly worsening physical condition soon discouraged him. Probably, towards the end of the stay in Formia, at the height of 1935, Gramsci started to give up. The temptation to "disappear like a stone in the ocean",[20] seems to prevail, from time to time coming to the fore, and this explains the end of the drafting of the *Quaderni* ("Notebooks"), and the thinning out of the letters; and lastly it explains the increasingly bitter the tone and the progressive emergence of a sentiment that he rejected in the past, self-pity: "this hell in which I am slowly dying".[21] He wrote in this way in 1933, months after the serious crisis that had struck him in March. From this point, though still managing to hold the pen in his hand, the following years were an ordeal. His last notes are from May 1935. During this period, he only wrote occasional letters to his family (with an increase of those to his children), while the relationship with his wife worsened, even though he continued in vain to urge her return to Italy. The transition to another clinic, the Quisisana of Rome, did not have the desired effects. His body was too worn out; the spirit had suffered too much. The period in Rome was inactive, in essence, while his fears, anxieties and sense of failure increased, and Giulia's expectation became self-deception.

Death arrived on April 27, 1937 and freed Gramsci from everything. As soon as he heard the news, Piero Sraffa was right to say, that it was "a disgrace without equal"[22] – not only for his friends and companions and for the story of world communism, but for the history of international culture.

Bibliography

Gramsci's Works and Abbreviations
Gramsci, A. (1994a), *Letters from Prison*, Rosengarten, F. (ed.), vol. 1 (New York: Columbia University Press).
Gramsci, A. (1994b), *Letters from Prison*, Rosengarten, F. (ed.), vol. 2 (New York: Columbia University Press).
LC: Caprioglio, S., Fubini, E. (eds.) (1965), *Lettere dal carcere* (Torino: Einaudi).
LC2: Santucci, A. (ed.) (1996), *Lettere dal carcere. 1926–1937* (Palermo: Sellerio).

---

20 Gramsci 1994b: 5, Gramsci to Giulia, January 13, 1931 (LC: 398; LC2: 387).
21 Gramsci 1994b: 308, Gramsci to Tania, July 6, 1933 (LC: 798; LT: 1320; LC2: 727).
22 Sraffa 1991: 180, Sraffa to Tatiana, April 27, 1937.

LT: Natoli, A., Daniele, C. (eds.) (1997), A. Gramsci, T. Schucht, *Lettere. 1926–1935* (Torino: Einaudi).

Q: Gerratana, V. (ed.) (1975), *Quaderni del carcere* (Torino: Einaudi), 4 vols.

SPN: Hoare, Q., Nowell-Smith, G. (eds.) (1971), *Selection from the Prison Notebooks* (New York: International Publishers).

Other Works

d'Orsi, A. (ed.) (2014), *Inchiesta su Gramsci. Quaderni scomparsi, abiure, conversioni, tradimenti: leggende o verità?* (Torino: Accademia University Press).

d'Orsi, A. (2018), *Gramsci. Una nuova biografia. Nuova edizione rivista e accresciuta* (Milano: Feltrinelli).

Fabre, G. (2015), *Lo scambio. Come Gramsci non fu liberato* (Palermo: Sellerio).

Francioni, G. (1984), *L'officina gramsciana. Ipotesi sulla struttura dei Quaderni del carcere* (Napoli: Bibliopolis).

Francioni, G. (2009), *Come lavorava Gramsci*, in Francioni, G. (ed.), *Quaderni del carcere. Edizione anastatica dei manoscritti* (Roma-Cagliari: Biblioteca Treccani-L'Unione Sarda).

Gerratana, V. (1997), *Gramsci. Problemi di metodo* (Roma: Editori Riuniti).

Giacomini, R. (2017), *Gramsci e il giudice* (Roma: Castelvecchi).

Sraffa, P. (1991), *Lettere a Tania per Gramsci*, Introduzione e cura di V. Gerratana (Roma: Editori Riuniti).

Stochino, G. (2016), *Gramsci al confino di Ustica: Due interviste raccolte da Giulia Stochino*, in "Gramsciana", 3, pp. 151–167.

Suppa, S. (2016), *Ordine e conflitto. Una trama per rileggere Gramsci* (Torino: Giappichelli).

Vacca, G. (2012), *Vita e pensieri di Gramsci. 1926–1937* (Torino: Einaudi).

PART 2

Theories of History

∵

CHAPTER 3

The Crisis of European Civilization in the Thought of Antonio Gramsci

Giuseppe Vacca

The First World War influenced the whole development of Gramsci's thought. For him, the war was the culminating manifestation of a crisis in European civilization that had been building since 1870. What distinguishes Gramsci from other important thinkers of his time is not just his capacity to identify the causes of Old Europe's decline, but his ability to intuit the features of the nascent "New World".

In describing the "world of yesterday" submerged by the war, Gramsci emphasizes the breakdown of the world market – something which to him seems "irremediable":

The war – he writes in "L'Ordine Nuovo" (The New Order) on November 8th, 1919 – has irretrievably broken the worldwide equilibrium of capitalistic production. Before the war, a dense network of trade relations had been established in the world. Economically speaking, the world had become like a living organism with blood coursing through its veins. The capitalists had accomplished a huge amount: for decades, millions of individuals driven by the desire for personal profit had worked in the world seeking relationships, fostering them in order to sustain a healthy variety of venous and arterial blood vessels (so to speak), through which the life of the world circulated with the pulses of a multiplicity of "hearts": the various large markets of production and consumption.[1]

This grandiose process, triggered by the vocation of capitalist production to unify the world, had happened "spontaneously" thanks to the economic energy of capitalism. The aim indicated by Gramsci in the *Quaderni del carcere* ("Prison Notebooks") was that of contributing to consciously creating the "conditions of an economy according to a worldwide plan". Along the way, his diagnosis of the crisis unfolds – leading from the analysis in real time of the war to his personal reflections found in the *Quaderni del carcere*. The war had not only destroyed the old checks and balances and the old civilization, it had also

---

1 Gramsci 1987: 303–304.

established a new world order: a hierarchy of power that immediately after the peace of Versailles he considers "catastrophic":

> The myth of war – the unity of the world in the League of Nations – was realized in ways and in the form that could be achieved under private and national property: in the monopoly of the globe exercised and exploited by the Anglo-Saxons. The economic and political life of the states is strictly controlled by Anglo-American capitalism [...]. It is the death of the state, which is, as it is sovereign and independent. National capitalism is reduced to the condition of a vassal [...]. The national state is dead: becoming a sphere of influence, a monopoly in the hands of foreigners. The world is "unified" in the sense that a world hierarchy has been created that the whole world regulates and controls authoritatively.[2]

These blazing insights springing from the war will, ten years later, coalesce into a true and proper theory of crises enunciated in a long note from February 1933,[3] specifically dedicated to the global economic crises of 1929–1932. Gramsci asks himself: "When did the crisis begin?" And he responds: "since this is a development and not an event, the issue is important. One can say that there is not beginning date for the crisis as such, but only of some more clamorous "manifestations" that are erroneously and tendentiously identified with the crisis". It is very significant that between the "tendentious" interpretations, he points out those which isolate the crash of the New York Stock Exchange, since they come from those that "want to find the origin and the cause of the crisis" in "Americanism". But we will return to this later. Here, it is worthwhile to dwell on the connection between the (economic) crisis and the war:

> All of the postwar period was a crisis, with attempts to prevent it, sometimes turning into good fortune in this or that country, but nothing else. For some (and perhaps not wrongly) the war itself was a manifestation of this crisis, indeed the first manifestation. The war was precisely the political and organizational response of those responsible for it.

This way of analyzing the crisis does not separate economic processes from the social antagonisms and political changes. The correlation between the crisis and war and the consideration of both as more "complicated" "manifestations" of historical processes linking the internal life of states to their position in

---

2 Gramsci 1987: 20.

3 FSPN: 219–220 (Q 15, § 5: 1755–1756).

international relations. Analyzing the first point, Gramsci reaches a more precise periodization of the crisis, giving emphasis to "issues" that had been ac-
cumulating inside of states starting from 1870. In June 1933, he wrote: "Every-
body recognizes that the war of 1914–1918 represents an historical break, in the
sense that a whole series of questions which piled up individually before 1914
have precisely formed a 'mound', modifying the general structure of the previous process". Gramsci enumerated these "questions" one by one, systematically
categorizing them as a "trade-union phenomenon", and between them he underlines the birth of the socialist movement, after which the progressive en-
trance of the subaltern classes into the life of the state had become a decisive
question.[4] Returning then to the chain of events between the origin of the crisis and that of the war, Gramsci's annotation of February 1933 reaches a complete formulation of the theory of these crises: the war, as much as the crisis,
had arisen from the "contradiction" between the cosmopolitanism of the economy and the "nationalism" of politics, intensifying during the "age of empires"
and culminating in the war:

> One of the fundamental contradictions is this: that whereas economic
> life has internationalism, or better still cosmopolitanism, as a necessary
> premiss, state life has developed ever more in the direction of "national-
> ism", of "self-sufficiency" and so on. One of the most apparent features of
> the "present crisis" is nothing other than the intensification of the nation-
> alistic element (nationalistic state element) in the economy: quota sys-
> tems, clearings, trading currency restrictions, balanced trading between
> two single states etc.[5]

Clearly, Gramsci does not predict a necessarily "catastrophic" outcome for the
crisis[6] and this constitutes its distinctive trait in the communism of the 1930s
(and not only). Above all, he indicates a way out with the condition that the
ruling class knows how to remove this asymmetry, creating new balances between the "space" of the economy and that of politics. Nevertheless, the ruling
classes are prevalently molded by national politics, and thus the leaders
are principally responsible for the war and economic crisis and are rendered

---

4   Cf. SPN: 106 (Q 15, § 59: 1824).

5   FSPN: 220 (Q 15, § 5: 1756).

6   "We might, then, say – and this would be more exact – that the 'crisis' is none other than the
    quantitative intensification of certain elements, neither new nor original, but in particular
    the intensification of certain phenomena, while others that were there before and operated
    simultaneously with the first, sterilizing them, have now became inoperative or have com-
    pletely disappeared" (ibid.)

increasingly more inept by the way in which the war and crisis impact the biggest creation of European modernity: the nation state. We must therefore look at the way in which Gramsci comes back to the theme of the crisis of the state in the *Prison Notebooks*.

The lexicon changes: he no longer speaks of "death" as he did in the 1920s, but of the "crisis" of the State and he does not only inflect it in relation to the exercise of sovereignty. Certainly, he is very attentive to new limitations of the sovereignty of State that he considers particularly negative, such as in the case of the Concordat,[7] but he does not recognize the strength of the State in the exercise of a (presumptuous) absolute territorial sovereignty, but rather in the capacity to open up to supranationality.

Before analyzing the solutions, it is worthwhile pondering the vision of the crisis of the State. Differently than the period immediately postwar when, as we have seen, the "death of the State" was attributed to prevalently exogenous factors, in the 1930s the emphasis falls on the "crisis of authority" of the traditional ruling classes, made even more serious by the incapacity of the subaltern classes to indicate a way out. In a note dating from December 1930, Gramsci calls attention to the changed behavior of important European intellectuals before the nascent society of the masses. He affirms: "Today, a phenomenon similar to that of the separation between the 'spiritual' and 'temporal' in the Middle Ages has occurred in the modern world: a much more complex phenomenon – he adds – than that of the past, more complex than modern life". This has, as a consequence, the loss of a fundamental contribution to the development of hegemony, as much as for the ruling classes as for the subaltern classes:

> regressive and conservative social groupings are shrinking back more and more to their initial economic-corporative phase, while progressive and innovative groupings are still in their initial phase – which is, precisely, the economic-corporative phase. The traditional intellectuals are detaching themselves from the social grouping to which they have hitherto given the highest, most comprehensive form and hence the most extensive and complete consciousness of the modern state. Their detachment is in fact an act of incalculable historical significance; they are signaling and sanctioning the crisis of the state in its decisive form.[8]

7   Cf. FSPN: 60–70 (Q 16, § 11: 1865–1874).
8   PN3: 8–9 (Q 6, § 10: 690–691).

The shot is aimed at Benedetto Croce, who in his speech given at the World Congress of Philosophy at Oxford, had denounced "a certain weakening and mental fading" caused by the war, heaping everything in to the same bundle: futurism and neoclassicism, imperialism and nationalism, "Marxist socialism, statism which heralds itself as 'ethical', the revival of the Catholic and clerical" (the reference is to the Concordat).[9] Gramsci urges: "Today, the 'spiritual' that is detaching itself from the 'temporal' and setting itself apart is something disorganic, decentered, an unstable scattering of great cultural personalities, 'without a Pope' and without territory".[10]

Croce, appeared to Gramsci to be moved by the intention of drawing up the "political manifesto for an international union of the great intellectuals of all countries, especially the Europeans", and he intuited "that this might become an important party and play a significant role";[11] thus, in the *Quaderno 10* ("Notebook 10") he defines Croce as the most effective "ideologist" of a "passive revolution" aimed at stopping the rise of the popular classes in Europe.[12] The crisis of European civilization is summarized then by the "disintegration of the modern State", that placed on the historical-political field, could give rise to different solutions, provided that old and new "social groupings" know how to lay the base of a new civilization. These can emerge from the dialectic between Europe and America that Gramsci considers very differently from ten years before, from the creation of a "European union" and lastly from a new direction of the international communist movement.

The rejection of anti-Americanism is widespread in the *Prison Notebooks*, where Gramsci judges Taylorism and Fordism as the vehicles of a more advanced industrial capitalism than that of Europe – more democratic and above all destined to accelerate the creation of "planned economy".[13] Arguing with Luigi Pirandello, who had judged the spreading of "Americanism" as dissonant against European custom "like the make-up on the face of an old prostitute", Gramsci asks himself

whether America, through the implacable weight of its economic production (and therefore indirectly), will compel or is already compelling Europe to overturn its excessively antiquated economic and social basis.

---

9   Gramsci was looking at the published text in the dossier of "La Critica" from November 20, 1930 with the title *Antistoricismo* (401–409).

10   PN3: 9 (Q 6, § 10: 691).

11   PN3: 8 (Q 6, § 10: 690).

12   Cf. SPN: 118–120 (Q 10, § 9: 1227–1229). On the concept of passive revolution cf. Vacca 2017: chapter II.

13   SPN: 279–280 (Q 22, § 1: 2139–2140).

This would have happened anyway, though only slowly. In the immediate perspective it is presented as a repercussion of American super-power. In other words, whether we are undergoing a transformation of the material bases of European civilization, which in the long run (though not all that long, since in the contemporary period everything happens much faster than in the pas ages) will bring about the overthrow of the existing forms of civilization and the forced birth of a new.[14]

Naturally, the prediction does not represent a proclamation in favor of the "Americanization" of Europe since Gramsci judges American civilization as primitive and basic ("hegemony is born in the factory", the "corporate-economic" prevails upon the "political-ethical", in the development of hegemony intellectual groups in America have a residual or subaltern role). In fact, Gramsci writes,

> it is not from the social groups "condemned" by the new order that reconstruction is to be expected, but from those on whom is imposed the burden of creating with their own suffering the material bases of the new order. It is they who "must" find for themselves an "original", and not Americanised, system of living to turn into "freedom" what today is "necessity".[15]

These statements take us back to the way in which Gramsci rethinks the future prospects of Communism, once the myth of "worldwide revolution" fades.[16] In concrete terms, he advocates the reorientation of international communism based on a realistic forecast of the possibilities that, driven by the unification of the world, can prevail over the "crisis". In this way he hopes for a "nationalization" of the communist parties with the aim of contributing to the reconstruction of a new world unity.[17] Gramsci's prediction is that the unification of

---

14   SPN: 317 (Q 22, § 15: 2178–2179). Gramsci commented on the Pirandello text in an interview with Corrado Alvaro published in "L'Italia letteraria", April 14th, 1929.

15   Ibid.

16   A theme that I cannot deal with here. Cf. Vacca 2017: chapter I.

17   SPN: 241 (Q 14, § 68: 1729): "A class that is international in character has – in as much as it guides social strata which are narrowly national (intellectuals), and indeed frequently even less than national: particularistic and municipalistic (the peasants) – to 'nationalise' itself in a certain sense. Moreover, this sense is not a very narrow one either, since before the conditions can be created for an economy that follows a world plan, it is necessary to pass through multiple phases in which the regional combinations (of groups of nations) may be of various kind" (July 1933).

the human race might move forward step by step through the "regionalization" of the world economy; and his aim is that the Communist movement redefines its mission, becoming the creator of a "type of modern cosmopolitanism". According to Gramsci, the "regionalization" of the world economy is a solid outlook and can make decisive strides in Europe:

> There is today – he writes in March of 1931 – a European cultural consciousness, and there exists a long list of public statements by intellectuals and politicians who maintain that a European union is necessary. It is fair to say that the course of history is heading toward this union and that there are many material forces that will only be able to develop within this union. If this union were to come into existence in x years, the word "nationalism" will have the same archaeological value as "municipalism" today.[18]

For Gramsci, therefore, the concept of "internationalism" seems to be anachronistic and misunderstood, in any case inappropriate to the Italian situation where "internationalism" was traditionally confused with the "subversion" of the subaltern classes.[19] Turning the negative meaning previously attributed to the term "cosmopolitanism" neatly on its head, he coins the concept of "a modern type of cosmopolitanism" in order to indicate in the working classes, the power that can "help to rebuild the world economically in a unitarian mode":

> Modern expansion is of a finance-capitalist kind. At present in Italy the element "man" is either "man-capital" or "man-labour". Italian expansion can only be that of "man-labour" and the intellectual who represents "man-labour" is not the traditional intellectuals, swollen with rhetoric and literary memories of the past. Traditional Italian cosmopolitanism should become a modern type of cosmopolitanism, one that can assure the best conditions for the development of Italian "man-labour" in whatever part of the world he happens to be. Not the citizen of the world as civis romanus os as Catholic, but as producer of civilization. One can therefore maintain that the Italian tradition is continued dialectically in the working people and their intellectuals, not in the traditional citizen and the traditional intellectual. The Italian people are the people with the greatest "national" interest in a modern form of cosmopolitanism. Not only the worker but also the peasant, especially the southern peasant.

---

18   SPN: 60–61 (Q 6, § 78: 748).
19   PN2: 45–47 (Q 3, § 46: 325–327), June-July 1930.

It is in the tradition of Italian people and Italian history to collaborate in rebuilding the world in an economically unified way not in order to dominate it hegemonically and appropriate the fruit of others' labour but to exist and develop precisely as the Italian people.[20]

In the first draft of the quoted passage dated November 1932, Gramsci had used the concept of "cosmopolitanism" and that of "internationalism" indifferently.[21] In the next draft he abandons the second term definitively, opting for the notion of "modern cosmopolitanism". His analysis then culminates in proposing the "nationalization" of the Italian Communist Party in order to "collaborate in the economic rebuilding of the world in a unified way". The remodeling of the national function of the working classes into a neo-cosmopolitan perspective, passing through the foreseeable supranational stages, projects Gramsci beyond the intellectual and political horizon of the 1930s.

Bibliography

Gramsci's Works and Abbreviations

Gramsci, A. [1919] (1987), *La settimana politica. Italia e Stati Uniti*, ("L'Ordine Nuovo", November 8), in Gramsci, A., *L'Ordine Nuovo 1919–1920*, Gerratana, V., Santucci, A.A. (eds.) (Torino: Einaudi).

CW: Forgacs, D., Nowell-Smith, G. (eds.) (1985), *Selections from Cultural Writings* (Cambridge, MA: Harvard University Press).

FSPN: Boothman, D. (ed.) (1995), *Further Selections from the Prison Notebooks* (Minneapolis: Minnesota University Press).

PN: Buttigieg, J.A. (ed.) (1992, 1996, 2007), *Prison Notebooks* (New York: Columbia University Press), 3 vols.

Q: Gerratana, V. (ed.) (1975), *Quaderni del carcere* (Torino: Einaudi), 4 vols.

---

20   CW: 246–247 (Q 19, § 5: 1988). This reflection immediately precedes a note dedicated to confuting the justification of the colonial politics of fascism that was searching for international legitimization citing overpopulation as cause of Italy's inferiority. Gramsci replied that the "relative poverty" of the Italian people was not derived from the demographic composition but from the unavailability of the "dominant economic class" to rationalize the production of the "international wealth" (FSPN: 237–239; Q 19, § 6: 1989–1991).

21   Cf. FSPN: 238–239 (Q 19, § 6; 1990–1991).

SPN: Hoare, Q., Nowell-Smith, G. (eds.) (1971), *Selection from the Prison Notebooks* (New York: International Publishers).

Other Works

Vacca, G. (2017), *Modernità alternative. Il Novecento di Antonio Gramsci* (Torino: Einaudi).

CHAPTER 4

Notes on Gramsci's Theory of History

Marcello Montanari

1   **The Critique of Historical Time between the Two World Wars**

In the work program that Gramsci outlined starting from March 1929, one of the proposed aims was to add to the development of a theory of history and historiography.[1] His intention was to liberate Marxism from a theory of historical time that was rigid and dominated by the logic of "before-after": a concept of time as a homogenous and absolute reality which develops outside of us – outside of our own will.

The need to reinvent the Marxist theory of history springs from the maturing of cultural orientation (in the post-war period after WWI), which tried to consider the discontinuity that the war had produced. The conviction that history proceeds "towards the best" begins to deteriorate. The war itself is a fracturing element of history: a dramatic interruption of Time that requires the reworking of new interpretive categories. This is the negation of every notion of linearity and rationality in history. It is the affirmation of a temporality without direction – without sense – completely against Newton's concept of "absolute" time, measured by clocks.

Right in front of him, Gramsci has Croce and not the Croce of *Teoria e storia della storiografia* ("Theory and History of Historiography") where the presence of "historical naturalism" is still strongly felt (a conception of history marked by "before-after"), but the Croce that founded a transcendental theory (or ethic) of freedom. He has Croce "the boss of revisionism" staring him in the face so to speak, as well as being the inspiring force of Bernstein's Marxism.[2] This obliges him to make a close comparison with the theory of value and, more generally, with the concept of historical time.

Through Croce, Gramsci tackles, above all, the themes that European culture was facing in order to rework the interpretative categories of its own time.

---

1 Cf. Gramsci 1994: 256, Gramsci to Tatiana, 25 March 1929 (LT: 333).
2 That fact that Croce had influenced Bernstein's research is documented in the letter written by Sorel to Croce dated September 9, 1899, where he writes: "Bernstein has just written me, that he indicated in 'Neue Zeit' n. 46 that he had been inspired, in a certain way, by your work" (Sorel 1980: 86).

He confronts the culture of crisis (the *finis Europae*) that reflects on the decline of the liberal age, its euro-centric and "Enlightenment" ideology. It is actually difficult to isolate Gramsci from the debate that developed around the "European crisis of conscience" during the 1920s and 1930s. There are many paths through which the European philosophical conscience notices that there is no "history in movement": a history that develops according to natural laws, that history does not have its own "immanent logic" and that it is no longer possible to follow a calm narration of the progressive historical becoming as was followed by Ranke or the "early" Meinecke.

There are, however, two moments that explicitly illustrate the changing horizon of European culture. These are: (*a*) the debate between Cassirer and Heidegger regarding "Kant's legacy" that took place in Davos in the spring of 1929 (we will return to this later); (*b*) the lessons held by Kojéve on Hegel's *Phänomenologie des Geistes* ("Phenomenology of Spirit"), where the theme is the definition of freedom as the negation of historical determination and, thus, the *positivity of the negative*. Gramsci ignores both the first and second moments, but it is with this "culture of crisis" that he makes an account, when, through the comment of the conference held by Croce at Oxford in September of 1930, he describes the process that brings the intellectuals to the point of separating from the national state in order to assume a supra-national function.[3] He sees all the drama of this separation of the "spiritual" from the "temporal". And in this he sees the "disintegration of the modern state" or, more precisely, that type of administrative and monarchic state structured on the foundation of political-military and economic control of a determined territory. It is, though, that process of separation from the intellectuals "from the social grouping to which they had previously given the highest and most comprehensive form" that breaks the temporality of modern history and gives birth to the "culture of crisis": a culture now deprived of its foundations (the Homeland, the People, Tradition).

To the necessity of overcoming the "Newtonian" concept of historical time – the understanding of time as a progressive accumulation of knowledge, resources and civil achievements – Gramsci arrives at another way: the analysis of Americanism and Fordism.

In an annotation found in *Quaderno 10* ("Notebook 10"), Gramsci tells us that, in order to fight "the law of the falling rate of profit", Ford "had to get out of the strictly industrial field of production to organize the transportation and distribution of his goods".[4] In this way, he changed the relationship between

---

3   Cf. PN3: 8–9 (Q 6, § 10: esp. 690–691).
4   FSPN: 431 (Q 10II, § 36: 1282).

the spheres of production and consumption. And it is starting from the change of this relationship that a mass society is created, or more precisely, a *democracy of consumption*: a society where access to consumption by the subaltern classes becomes one of the principle criteria for the organization of society. Inside such a social form, the *conflictual participation* of the working class in the government of capitalistic development is plausible and fully justifiable. But the most relevant fact (and that is why it is so important for the definition of a theory of history) is that, with the changing relationship between production and consumption, the characters of the principal social figures also change. New and unexpected social figures are formed and grow in this new environment. Productive activity incorporates and attracts increasingly more refined forms of knowledge and the relationship between work time and free time changes to the point that even "free time" (or non-work time) becomes the moment of the total reproduction of values. The *reductio ad unum* of the processing times of goods becomes very unlikely: their measurability according to absolute time becomes improbable. It is the same as David Ricardo's idea of working time as a measure of the value of the goods to be considered. Ricardo could imagine measuring the value of goods on the basis of the amount of work time it took to create them, because it presupposed the existence of absolute and continuous time. But the multiplication of different types of concrete work and the growing diversification of knowledge embedded in them makes them hardly traceable only to the goods-labor force delivered in the last phase of the production process. The productive *abstract work* of value identifies with the entire system of knowledge and with *work as together.* On the contrary, it is the different quality and types of knowledge incorporated in the production process that enhances goods in a differentiated. The result is a decline in the so-called "centrality of the working class" and its "revolutionary" function.

Changing the relationship between production and consumption and exiting "from the strictly industrial field of production", one could say that Ford re-unified capital and knowledge and *reduced* the role and social impact of factory work. If the formula of the tendential decline of the rate of profit (pv/c+v) says that profit decreases with the growth of constant capital, Ford found the way to contextually devalue the variable capital, in way that the total value of this formula would remain unchanged. The formula of "tendential decline" presupposes that variable capital remain *invariable* with the growth of the constant capital, but it is exactly this that *does not occur* because the incorporation of knowledge into production (establishing a stronger unity between capital and knowledge or, between "bourgeois" and "intellectuals") tends to "devalue" the function of work in the final phase of production and, at the same time, render the reproduction of the work force – in virtue of the over-abundance of goods produced – less onerous for the capital.

What happens, then, is that with Fordism, the value of work time tends to decrease. And with this decrease, the same centrality of the work time in the underlining of social processes of accumulation of riches declines. The perception of the forms of becoming changes; both the perception and the concept of time change. A new theory of historical becoming becomes indispensable. It is not by chance that in *Quaderno 10* ("Notebook 10") Gramsci's notes on Croce intertwine with those on Ricardo and the notes on the theory of history with the notes on the theory of value. Ricardo, in fact, is thought of more as a philosopher than as an economist, because, in order to conceptualize work time in new ways as a measure of labor means to conceptualize the same historical time in a new way.

In European culture between the two World Wars, the image of absolute time – homogenous and continuous – is broken (an idea that can be traced to Ricardo and Newton). It is the sign of the decline of Europe's faith in itself and its own history lived and thought of as the journey of the human race towards a world liberated from darkness – as a progressive "enlightening" or as an unstoppable process of the rationalization of human life. One must read *Quaderno 10* ("Notebook 10" – the criticism of "the religion of freedom") and *Quaderno 11* ("Notebook 11" – the criticism of historical determinism-naturalism) having clearly in mind that in these are expressed the awareness that Americanism had changed the structure of time and that after the Great War, such a structural change had been intertwined with the crisis of the European historical conscience. At the center of a new theory of history, there must be then the idea of a passage from absolute time to "relative" time: from the linearity and progression of time to an image of time as discontinuous and inhomogeneous form.

From this point, originates Bukharin's criticism of "historical materialism". A criticism that has two focal points:
a) the concept of objective reality and therefore of the predictability of historical becoming;
b) the idea of the translatability scientific languages.

2   Criticism of Bukharin. Objectivity and Translatability

From the pages that Gramsci dedicates to the criticism of Bukharin's historical materialism in *Quaderno 11* ("Notebook 11"), clearly emerges that for him "objective" means *humanly* objective. "Man – he writes – knows objectively in so far as knowledge is real for the whole human race *historically* unified in a single unitary cultural system. [...] There exists therefore a struggle for objectivity [...] and this struggle is the same as the struggle for the cultural unification of the uman race".[5] The objective knowledge of "reality" (that which is historical or "natural" and is external to us) is connected to our subjectivity and to our capacity to communicate with others, through a formal and linguistic system, which is our perception of reality; the very idea that an external world independent from our capacity to formulate cognitive models (knowledge, interpretations, languages) is negated. Objectivity exists in the possibility to communicate and therefore to translate logical-linguistic representations into other languages (the paradigm or algorithm) of the "object of knowledge" that we construct.

This concept of objectivity excludes the idea that human appropriation of nature and historical becoming can be indicated by "natural laws" that are pre-existent to human intentionality. These laws are none other than cognitive models that enable us to give form and order to the world which surrounds us. In any case, between our knowledge and our "inner reality" (between the "object of knowledge" and the "object in oneself") there is no difference. It follows that the two terms of the man-nature relationship (or individual-historical sphere) reciprocally imply each other. In this relationship, there is nothing that transcends human intentionality: there is no "nature" or "historical movement" that have their own temporality and existence beyond knowledge and human creations. For this reason, one can say that there is nothing mechanical or automatic in historical becoming. There is nothing "in nature" conceivable as an absolutely transcendent reality or as an elusive "in one self" with respect to the practical-cognitive intentionality of humankind.

It is this particular vision of "objectivity" that brings us to the Davos debate between Cassirer and Heidegger.[6] Two different visions of philosophy (and of the history of philosophy) clash in Davos. A difference that Heidegger makes explicit, asking the question: "to what extent does philosophy have the task of freeing ourselves from anguish? Or does it not have the task of radically delivering the man to it?".[7] The discussion is about Kant. But in the background is the reading of the crisis of European consciousness. A crisis that, for Heidegger, indicates the impossibility of man-entity to produce knowledge that permits him to transcend his own finiteness and autonomously handle his own

---

5   SPN: 445 (Q 11, § 17: 1416).
6   The debate is reported in an appendix to Heidegger 1981. Cf. also Cassirer, Heidegger 1990.
7   Heidegger 1981: 228.

historical destiny. For Cassirer, it is a crisis that fails to discuss the fundamental principal of Western cultural tradition: the idea that human reason possesses all the potential to produce knowledge and symbolic forms as well as to govern his own existence and plan his own future.

What does Heidegger claim at Davos? He affirms that, in the passage from the first to the second edition of *Critique of Pure Reason*, Kant theorizes in the face of the finiteness of man and human knowledge and turns to more acceptable questions for traditional metaphysics. For this reason, Kant would have muted the theme of "transcendental imagination" (or "faculty of imagination") and would have accepted the finiteness of being and its imperfect capacities for producing knowledge. He definitely would have accepted to subordinate "being" to the unspeakable and absolute otherness of being. He would have resized and closed "being" in its finiteness – in its *"being in time"*.

Against this interpretation, Cassirer negates Kant's recession on more orthodox and traditional positions and instead affirms that in the Kantian reflection the "transcendental imagination" (the capacity to imagine and construct objects of knowledge and/or to produce symbolic forms) assumes a central function, signaling the passage – realized in the *Kritik der praktischen Vernunft* ("Critique of Practical Reason") – of the search for formal conditions for the production of knowledge defined as "transcendental freedom" as the capacity to imagine a "must be". Cassirer deduces being to its finiteness (to its determination in space and time) and makes "transcendental freedom" the capacity to break the determinations of "absolute time"; where Heidegger had reduced freedom of "being" to the interrogation of the Being.

In Cassirer's reading of Kant, the idea of objectivity as "humanly objective" or of knowledge as imagination and as a construction of an "object of knowledge" recurs. The criticism of every naturalism and/or historical determinism also recurs. "Reality" (both historical and natural) is seen as constructed by our transcendent faculty of imagining the object of knowledge, as well as by our faculty of giving material existence to that "must be" that our transcendental imagination (or cognitive faculty) has allowed us to construct. According to Cassirer, the fundamental problem of Kant is not the relationship between *Being and Time* but between *Being and Must Be*. Fundamentally, if for Heidegger the constitutive element of being is Time (it is thrown into Time; overdetermined by time, dominated and dissolved in absolute Time), for Cassirer time is subordinate, articulated by our transcendental freedom; by our capacity to construct *symbolic forms* (languages, knowledge, culture, institutions). In this way, Heidegger appears to be a pure *determinist*: nothing happens unless it was predetermined; nothing happens that was not already placed in absolute, linear and homogeneous temporality that transcends and overwhelms everything with an inescapable force. Cassirer, on the other hand, speaks of the human capacity to invent unpredictable figures and relational systems.

These are two decidedly different readings of the crisis. One tells us: "put your faith in the Being". The other: "we need to affirm our transcendental freedom". And, with these due differences, it is the latter which constitutes the nucleus of the theoretical position that Croce expresses in *Storia d'Europa* ("History of Europe"). Gramsci moves forward from this idea of transcendental freedom, even if he highlights its limits. I would be tempted to say that Bukharin (along with a substantial part of Western Marxism) is on Heidegger's side. He thinks the existence of a temporality external to us is regulated by its own laws and mechanisms. He thinks that historical time is inescapable and that it overwhelms us. Bukharin does not accept the passage that Kant performs from determining judgement to reflective judgment and transcendental freedom. For him, all is necessitated and determined by historical laws. But in this way, history is an expression of transcendental freedom that is negated. The idea of laws which determine historical becoming refers to an absolutization of time: a temporality that, by canceling that transcendental freedom which allows one to imagine the "must be", in fact creates *anti-historicism* inasmuch as one negates the possibility of articulating time according to the political will and initiative of a determined subjectivity. *Anti-historicism* is created inasmuch as one thinks that the eternal laws of story can lead automatically to the liberation of humankind.

If Bukharin is on Heidegger's side, we say that Gramsci is with Cassirer. In my opinion, it is this which makes his critique of Croce's "religion of freedom" even more radical. For Cassirer, transcendental imagination is the source of ethical life, as it consents to think the "must be". The transition goes from "transcendental imagination" to "transcendental freedom", which considers the "must be". Gramsci's historicism has its roots in this vision of freedom as the capacity of the subject to imagine the "must be" and to base an ethic, or better yet, a practical initiative on this "imagination". It is this imagination, this capacity of practical initiative, which interrupts linear, homogenous, absolute time.

On this foundation, Gramsci can critique Croce's "religion of freedom" and consider it as a limited religion for only the wise and intellectual *élite*. Croce of the *Storia d'Europa* ("History of Europe"), in fact, while theorizing transcendental freedom and thinking about the non-linearity of historical time, it not able to think about the possibility of overcoming the division between leaders and followers. It is not enough to say that freedom is the fundamental power of history. One must add that this is the capacity to imagine and to create - on the basis of the translatability of languages – a "system of *communication*" that culturally reunifies humankind. And, failing to think of such a cultural reunification, Croce's principle of freedom can only appear to Gramsci as intrinsically limited.

3   On the Morphological Prediction

The criticism of Bukharin's determinism clarifies the Gramscian concept of "morphological prediction". Such criticism excludes that there can be an objective prediction based on "absolute time". The nexus of imagination and transcendental freedom, interrupting absolute and continuous time, does what need to be done so that there can no longer be an immediate cause-effect or before-after relationship. Time breaks away from freedom and history becomes predictable only on the basis of an intentionality, or more exactly, when one can predict only what one does. As Vico says, history is known and predicted only because we ourselves create it. It is expected to the extent that it operates. There is no purely objective prediction. "It is absurd – writes Gramsci – to think of a purely 'objective' prediction. Anybody who makes a prediction has in fact a 'programme' for whose victory he is working, and his prediction is precisely an element contributing to that victory".[8] Historical reality and its predictability are the products of our capacity to imagine and create the future. There is no "history in movement" that is independent from our will. And, in fact, historical determinism is linked to the absence of political initiative.

Within this frame, the theme of the relationship between causality and teleology, a theme which the political culture of the Second International had debated at length,[9] can be set in the terms of the constitution of a new subjectivity. It is the formation of an active subjectivity able to put the historical process in motion. There is no "history without actors". In the present economic-social formation, this subjectivity is the capital that incorporates knowledge and leading functions and addresses social growth as a whole. The formation of a different ("alternative") subject requires the invention of new forms of communication-relations between concrete works in a way that these "as a group" can become the "managers of the economy". This requires the creation of cultural and political devices needed to develop the translatability of languages and to promote their unification. This is the problem that, according to Gramsci, only the philosophy of praxis has placed in an organic way. The possibility that such a new subjectivity can emerge is justified by the idea that history is

---

8   SPN: 171 (Q 15, § 50: 1810).
9   On this debate see the remarkable observations of Racinaro 1976.

the history of freedom: history of that transcendental freedom, which is the will to interrupt linearity of absolute, linear and homogenous time, and has the ability to modify and reinvent the "symbolic forms" that order our life.

Bibliography

Gramsci's Works and Abbreviations

Gramsci, A. (1994), *Letters from prison*, vol. 1, Rosengarten, F. (ed.) (New York: Columbia University Press).

FSPN: Boothman, D. (ed.) (1995), *Further Selections from the Prison Notebooks* (Minneapolis: Minnesota University Press).

LT: Natoli, A., Daniele, C. (eds.) (1997), *A. Gramsci, T. Schucht, Lettere. 1926–1935* (Torino: Einaudi).

PN: Buttigieg, J.A. (ed.) (1992, 1996, 2007), *Prison Notebooks* (New York: Columbia University Press), 3 vols.

Q: Gerratana, V. (ed.) (1975), *Quaderni del carcere* (Torino: Einaudi), 4 vols.

SPN: Hoare, Q., Nowell-Smith, G. (eds.) (1971), *Selection from the Prison Notebooks* (New York: International Publishers).

Other Works

Cassirer, E., Heidegger, M. (1990), *Disputa sull'eredità kantiana. Due documenti (1928 e 1931)* (Milano: Unicopli).

Heidegger, M. (1981), *Kant e il problema della metafisica* (Bari: Laterza).

Racinaro, R. (1976), *Introduzione*, in Adler, M., *Causalità e teleologia nella disputa sulla scienza* (Bari: De Donato).

Sorel, G. (1980), *Lettere a Benedetto Croce* (Bari: De Donato).

CHAPTER 5

The Layers of History and the Politics in Gramsci

Vittorio Morfino

To speak of "layers of history" in Gramsci, or, in the terms I have given to the problem in recent years, of "plural temporality", means confronting one of the most powerful readings of Gramsci: Althusser's reading in *L'objet du "Capital"* ("The Object of '*Capital*'"), where Gramsci plays the paradigmatic role of absolute historicism, whose fundamental error consists in allowing Marxist history to lapse into an ideological concept of history that is dominated by the categories of continuity and contemporaneity, thus flattening the plurality of social levels into a uniform and homogenous present.[1] Of course, Althusser's reading of Gramsci has solicited numerous reactions. Among these, two worth remembering are Portantiero's *Los usos de Gramsci*,[2] and Thomas' *The Gramscian Moment*,[3] which have as a common denominator the centrality of the concept of "conjuncture". Their critique of Althusser is thus carried out by installing the concept of "conjuncture" (understood as the intertwining of temporality) at the heart of Gramscian thought. Whereas the contemporaneity of the present is what for Althusser renders politics unthinkable as a necessary expression of *that* present, it is precisely this intertwining of temporalities that opens onto a conception of politics as intervention in the conjuncture. In both cases, however, the concept of "conjuncture" which is wielded as a response to Althusser's criticism is precisely an Althusserian one, albeit nuanced, in Portaniero's case by the reference to Marx's 1857 *Einleitung*, and in Thomas' by the reference to Derrida's *Spectres de Marx* ("Specters of Marx"). For both authors, "conjuncture" does not signify a superficial variation of a fundamental structural invariance, but rather articulation: a complex intertwining of temporality. On the basis of these suggestions, it is necessary to return to Gramsci's text in order to measure the plausibility of a reading which poses the concept of a multiplicity of temporality at the center of his thought.

First, however, it will be necessary to consider some passages of Gramscian thought which explicitly move in the opposite direction, namely, in the direction of a unilinear, stagist, and progressive history. The influence of the 1859

---

1   Althusser 2015: 215–356.
2   Cf. Portantiero 1981.
3   Cf. Thomas 2009.

Vorwort ("Preface") that Gramsci translated while in prison[4] plays a key role in these texts. This text is extremely important within Marx's entire theoretical output, setting out the fundamental concepts of historical materialism (productive forces, relations of production, base, superstructure, revolution, and mode of production) in an extremely concise way. Furthermore, Marx speaks openly of "progressive Epochen",[5] miming *en matérialiste* the sequence of Hegelian kingdoms of spirit. Just as it is in the *Manifest der Kommunistischen Partei* ("The Communist Manifesto") – another text whose first chapter Gramsci translated in prison – revolution is the effect of the contradiction between productive forces and relations of production, and just like the *Manifest*, Marx uses the metaphor of pregnancy in order to explain the formation of a society within the one that precedes it.[6] However, two clauses are added which have the function of explaining the great defeats of 1848, which once again put the idea of revolution on the agenda in the moment of an ebb:

> no social order is ever destroyed before all the productive forces for which it is sufficient have been developed and new superior relations of production never replace older ones before the material conditions for their existence have matured within the framework of the old society. Mankind thus inevitably sets itself only such tasks as it is able to solve, since closer examination will always show that the problem itself arises only when the material conditions for its solution are already present or at least in the course of formation.[7]

It is a passage in which the stageist, deterministic, and teleological character is even accentuated.

In the *Quaderni del carcere* ("Prison Notebooks"), this passage is quoted "several times, first by heart, and then on the basis of Gramsci's own translation".[8] The first occurrence at Q 4, § 38 shows the measure of the theoretical importance Gramsci attributes to it:

> *Relations between structure and superstructures.* This is the crucial problem of historical materialism, in my view. Basics for finding one's bearings: 1) the principle that "no society sets itself tasks for the accomplishment

---

4 Gramsci 2007: 747.
5 Marx 1974: 9.
6 Marx, Engels 1959: 467.
7 Marx 1974: 9.
8 Frosini 2009: 662.

of which the necessary and sufficient solutions do not yet exist" [...] and 2) that "no society perishes until it has first developed all the forms of life implicit in its internal relations".[9]

For Gramsci, Marx's arguments become "the two principles of historical materialism" whose dialectical mediation resides in the concept of "permanent revolution".[10] Not only that, but as Gramsci maintains in Q 15, § 17, the concept of "passive revolution" is also derived from these principles:

> the concept of passive revolution must be rigorously derived from the two fundamental principles of political science: 1) that no social formation disappears as long as the productive forces which have developed within it still find room for further forward movement; 2) that a society does not set itself tasks for whose solution the necessary conditions have not already been incubated, etc.[11]

It is here, however, that Gramsci adds a precautionary remark of fundamental importance: "it goes without saying that these principles must first be developed critically in all their implications, and purged of every residue of mechanicism and fatalism".[12]

According to Gramsci, "development" and "purification" must be understood in the sense of reading these principles in tandem with the notion of the relation of forces.

However, before taking the argument in this direction, it is useful to consider a criticism Althusser addresses to Gramsci in a 1978 text, *Que faire?*, which has at its center precisely the relation between the "two principles" of the 1859 Preface and the concept of passive revolution. According to Althusser, the passage from Marx that Gramsci synthesizes into two "principles" cannot be explained except as a "survival of a philosophy of history [*survivance d'une philosophie de l'histoire*]",[13] which Gramsci would translate into a normative philosophy of history, wherein the category of revolution would be bifurcated into "normal" and "pathological" forms.

---

9   PN2: 177 (Q 4, § 38: 455). As Frosini notes, Gramsci recalls and cites this passage in several other places in the *Quaderni del carcere* ("Prison Notebooks"): PN3: 158 (Q 7, § 4: 855); PN3: 171 (Q 7, § 20: 869); PN3: 346 (Q 8, § 195: 1057); SPN: 367 (Q 10II, § 6: 1244); SPN: 432 (Q 11, § 22: 1422); SPN: 177 (Q 13, § 17: 1579); SPN: 106 (Q 15, § 17: 1774).

10 PN2: 178 (Q 4, § 38: 456–457).

11 SPN: 106 (Q 15, § 17: 1774).

12 SPN: 106–107 (Q 15, § 17: 1774).

13 Althusser 1978: 47.

Althusser's critique allows us to sketch a limit-form of Gramsci's thought where economic determinism gives way to a concept of politics understood as permanent revolution, whether active or passive. It is a philosophy of history which forbids any reference to a plural temporality, precisely because it is constructed on a unique, simple time of which all other times would be nothing but measurable variations on the normal-pathological axis. In this sense, Gramsci's own concept of "Caesarism" has an entire series of gradations, which can be measured on this axis.

Now, precisely in opposition to this limit-form, it is a matter of allowing "another" Gramsci to emerge. For this task, a fundamental passage is Q 11II, § 12, "Appunti per una introduzione e un avviamento allo studio della filosofia e della storia della cultura" ("The Study of Philosophy"). The opening is famous, with the claim that "all men are 'philosophers'",[14] where the quotation marks indicate that this statement is about "spontaneous philosophy",

> [this] is contained in: 1) in language itself, which is a totality of determined notions and concepts and not just of words grammatically devoid of content; 2) "common sense" and "good sense"; 3) popular religion and, therefore, also in the entire system of beliefs, superstitions, opinions, ways of seeing things and of acting, which are collectively bundled together under the name of "folklore".[15]

This "spontaneous philosophy" is philosophy insofar as it contains a conception of the world, but it is spontaneous insofar as it is "unconscious" or "unaware". Actually, however – and here our question comes into play – the difference is not only on the level of awareness, since it is precisely the moment Gramsci calls "critical awareness" which allows the fundamental character of "spontaneous philosophy" to emerge, that is, "broken and occasional" being:

> is it better to "think" without having critical awareness, in a disjointed and episodic way? In other words, is it better to take part in a conception of the world mechanically imposed by the external environment, i.e. by one of the many social groups in which everyone is automatically involved from the moment of his entry into the conscious world (and this can be one's village or province); it can have its origins in the parish and the "intellectual activity" of the local priest or aging patriarch whose wisdom is law, or in the little old woman who has inherited the lore of the

---

14   SPN: 323 (Q 11, § 12: 1375).
15   Ibid.

witches or the minor intellectual soured by his own stupidity and inability to act)? Or, on the other hand, is it better to work out consciously and critically one's own conception of the world and thus [...] take an active part in the creation of the history of the world, be one's own guide, refusing to accept passively and supinely from outside the moulding of one's personality?[16]

The alternative between unconscious spontaneous philosophy and conscious critical philosophy seems to be played out on the grounds of the limit-form of Gramsci's thought to which I alluded: activity or passivity with respect to a vision of world history whose path appears to be established. And yet, precisely at this point there emerges a theoretical element that destroys this simple alternative. The heteronomy is "mechanically imposed by an external environment", but, far from being permeated by a homogenous present, this is actually made up of a plurality of temporalities. In note I Gramsci adds:

In acquiring one's conception of the world one always belongs to a particular grouping which is that of all the social elements which share the same mode of thinking and acting. We are all conformists of some conformism or other, always man-in-the-mass or collective man. The question is this: of what historical type is the conformism, the mass humanity to which one belongs? When one's conception of the world is not critical and coherent but disjointed and episodic, one belongs simultaneously to a multiplicity of mass human groups. The personality is strangely composite: it contains Stone Age elements and principles of a more advanced science, prejudices from all past phases of history at the local level and intuitions of a future philosophy which will be that of a human race united the world over. To criticize one's own conception of the world means therefore to make it coherent unity and to raise it to the level reached by the most advanced thought in the world. It therefore also means criticism of all previous philosophy, in so far as this has left stratified deposits in popular philosophy. The starting-point of critical elaboration is the consciousness of what one really is, and is "knowing thyself" as a product of the historical process to date which has deposited in you an infinity of traces, without leaving an inventory.[17]

---

16   SPN: 323–324 (Q11, § 12: 1375–1376).
17   SPN: 324 (Q 11, § 12: 1376).

It is undeniable that in these passages there is a reference to the uniquely progressive time of *Weltgeschichte*, where not only is the present phase fixed, but also the one to come, that of the "globally unified humankind". Yet what is most interesting here is the plurality of temporalities that traverse individuals and social groups: the simultaneity of a plurality of times – a simultaneity which paradoxically means coexistence, but not co-presence. This plural temporality, not present in person in Gramsci's text, is indicated by a series of terms: "stratification", "anachronism", "fossil". A prime and privileged example is language:

> If it is true that every language contains the elements of a conception of the world and of a culture, it could also be true that from anyone's language one can assess the greater or lesser complexity of his conception of the world. Someone who only speaks dialect, or understands the standard language incompletely, necessarily has an intuition of the world which is more or less limited and provincial, which is fossilised and anachronistic in relation to the major currents of thought which dominate world history. His interests will be limited, more or less corporate or economistic, not universal. While it is not always possible to learn a number of foreign languages in order to put oneself in contact with other cultural lives, it is at the least necessary to learn the national language properly. A great culture can be translated into the language of another great culture, that is to say a great national language with historic richness and complexity, and it can translate any other great culture and can be a world-wide means of expression. But a dialect cannot do this.[18]

A second example is furnished by philosophy: "what must next be explained is how it happens that in all periods there co-exist many systems and currents of philosophical thought, how these currents are born, how they are diffused, and why in the process of diffusion they fracture along certain lines and in certain directions".[19] A third example is constituted by religion:

> every religion, even Catholicism [...] is in reality a multiplicity of distinct and often contradictory religions: there is one Catholicism for the peasants, one for *petits-bourgeois* and town workers, one for women, and one for intellectuals which is itself variegated and disconnected. But common sense is influenced not only by the crudest and least elaborated forms of these sundry Catholicisms as they exist today. Previous religions have also

---

18   SPN: 325 (Q 11, § 12: 1377).
19   SPN: 327 (Q 11, § 12: 1379).

had an influence and remain components of common sense to this day, and the same is true of previous forms of present Catholicism-popular heretical movements, scientific superstitions connected with past cults, etc.[20]

In Q 27, we then find some interesting reflections on folklore that Gramsci proposes to study as "a 'conceptions of the world and life' implicit to a large extent in determinate (in time and space) strata of society and in opposition [...] to 'official' conceptions of the world (or, in a broader sense, the conceptions of the cultured parts of historically determinate societies) that have succeeded one another in the in historical process".[21] He adds:

> This conception of the world is not elaborated and systematic because, by definition, the people (the sum total of the instrumental and subaltern classes of every form of society that has so far existed) cannot possess conceptions which are elaborated, systematic and politically organized and centralized in their albeit contradictory development. It is, rather, many-sided – not only because it includes different and juxtaposed elements, but also because it is stratified, from the more crude to the less crude – if, indeed, one should not speak of a confused agglomerate of fragments of all the conceptions of the world and of life that have succeeded one another in history. In fact, it is only in folklore that one finds surviving evidence, adulterated and mutilated, of the majority of these conceptions.[22]

"Multiple" and "stratified". The multiplicity and stratification of temporality is not deposited in the masses as successive degrees of a history of spirit recapitulated by a full present, but rather linked to a double materiality: the materiality of the trace and the materiality of practice. In other words, bodies are traced by this multiplicity of temporality through language, folklore, common sense, religion, and philosophy, giving rise to "bizarre", "incoherent", "composite", and "heteroclite" conceptions of the world. The trace, or better, traces, is the name of plural temporality in Gramsci: traces of practices that produce practices.

In his *Esquisse du concept de temps historique* ("Outline of a Concept of Historical Time"), Althusser claims that the conception of the Marxist social

---

20   SPN: 420 (Q 11, § 13: 1397).
21   CW: 189 (Q 27, § 1: 2311).
22   Ibid.

whole is characterized by a relative autonomy of different singular levels, and endowed with a differential temporality. Gramsci's text gives us a further indication: not only must a contemporaneity which traverses all levels of society be refused, but each single level is also non-contemporaneous. It is structurally affected by a plurality of times, which is, so to speak, an originary given, or what precedes any linearity or stagist aspect.

Of course, this Gramscian conception is linked closely to the rewriting of Thesis VI as well as of the relation between structure and superstructure in terms of economic, political, and military relations of force. In particular, in Q 13, § 17, after explaining the three degrees or moments of political relations of force, Gramsci writes:

> In real history these moments imply each other reciprocally horizontally and vertically, so to speak – i.e. according to socioeconomic activity (horizontally) and to country (vertically), combining and diverging in various ways. Each of these combinations may be represented by its own organized economic and political expression. It is also necessary to take into account the fact that international relations intertwine with these internal relations of nation-states, creating new, unique and historically concrete combinations. A particular ideology, for instance, born in a highly developed country, is disseminated in less developed countries, impinging on the local interplay of combinations. This relation between international forces and national forces is further complicated by the existence within every State of several structurally diverse territorial sectors, with diverse relations of force at all levels.[23]

In the beginning, methodologically, there is plurality: the plurality of temporality, a plurality that of course also affects spatiality. However, this plurality is not a disseminated plurality – it is not plurality understood in the postmodern sense. Instead, it is a plurality in which the "combination" dominates, whose "local game" is influenced by the international-national nexus. Far from placing social formations on a single and progressive timeline, where, as Marx says in the *Vorwort zur ersten Auflage* of *Das Kapital* ("Preface to the first edition" of "Capital"), advanced societies indicate "the image of their future"[24] to others,

---

23   SPN: 182 (Q 13, § 17: 1585).
24   With regard to the relationship between England and Germany, Marx writes the following: "the most industrially developed country [*entwickelter Land*] only shows the least developed one [*minder entwickelten*] the image of its future" (Marx 1962: 12).

Gramscian history consists of an original plurality of temporality, whatever the level of observation we are facing: individual, social group, nation, international scene. A conception of temporality clearly linked to the Gramscian question of the "molecular".

But plurality is not Gramsci's final word, because the concept of hegemony is what allows us to bring this plurality back, if not to the unity of a "History", then at least to a process of unification, that is, of a complex and conflictual articulation of a given plurality in which hegemonic apparatuses and intellectuals play a fundamental role. The Gramscian name of the result of these processes of unification is "historical bloc". Unity and contemporaneity are therefore always given as a temporary effect – relative and contingent – as a stabilization of a relationship of forces that is constitutively open and traversed, traced by other temporalities. And it seems to me that this is the sense of the Gramscian interpretation of the Marxist concept of permanent revolution.

Bibliography

Gramsci's Works and Abbreviations

Gramsci, A. (2007), *Quaderni del carcere 1. Quaderni di traduzioni (1929–1932)*, Cospito, G., Francioni, G. (eds.) (Roma: Istituto dell'Enciclopedia Italiana).

CW: Forgacs, D., Nowell-Smith, G. (eds.) (1985), *Selections from Cultural Writings* (Cambridge, MA: Harvard University Press).

PN: Buttigieg, J.A. (ed.) (1992, 1996, 2007), *Prison Notebooks* (New York: Columbia University Press), 3 vols.

Q: Gerratana, V. (ed.) (1975), *Quaderni del carcere* (Torino: Einaudi), 4 vols.

SPN: Hoare, Q., Nowell-Smith, G. (eds.) (1971), *Selection from the Prison Notebooks* (New York: International Publishers).

Other Works

Althusser, L. (1978), *Que faire?* (Unpublished MSS – Imec archive, ALT2. A26-05.06/07).

Althusser, L. (2015), *The Object of Capital*, in Althusser, L., Balibar, É., Establet, R., Macherey, P., Rancière, J., *Reading Capital: The Complete Edition* (London: Verso), pp. 215–356.

Frosini, F. (2009), *Prefazione del '59*, in Liguori, G., Voza, P., *Dizionario gramsciano 1926–1937* (Roma: Carocci).

Marx, K., Engels, F. (1959), *Manifest der Kommunistischen Partei*, in Marx, K., Engels, F., *Werke* (Berlin: Dietz), Bd. 4.

Marx, K. (1962), *Das Kapital,* in Marx, K., Engels, F., *Werke* (Berlin: Dietz), Bd. 23.

Marx, K. (1974), *Vorwort,* to *Zur Kritik der Politischen Ökonomie,* in Marx, K., Engels, F., *Werke* (Berlin: Dietz), Bd. 13.

Portantiero, J.C. (1981), *Los usos de Gramsci* (México D.F.: Folios Ediciones).

Thomas, P. (2009), *The Gramscian Moment* (Boston-Leiden: Brill).

PART 3

Communism

∴

CHAPTER 6

Gramsci's Antidogmatic Reading of Marx

Stefano Petrucciani

The connecting thread of this contribution is the following question: what are the distinctive features of the way Gramsci discusses Marx's thought? And in which traits does his approach differ from the ones of the many thinkers and political leaders that, in the twentieth century, accorded to Marx a central place in their reflections?

1   Gramsci's First Encounter with Marx's Thought

The first point to consider, as it is crucial for retracing the development of Gramsci's relation with Marx's thought, is the following: the Italian thinker always kept himself extremely far from the sanctification and dogmatization of Marx, that, on the contrary, undermines much of the socialist and communist readings of the German philosopher. Gramsci is fortunately immune from this disease, as his philosophical education, so strongly centered on the study of Italian idealism (Gentile and, above all, Croce), caused his first encounter with Marx to be in the spirit of uncoerced intellectual freedom. The young Gramsci, imbued with idealistic and anti-positivistic culture, did not hesitate to point out what he saw as the limits and flaws of Marx's thought in his famous essays of 1917 and 1918 – *La rivoluzione contro il Capitale* ("The Revolution against Capital"), *Il nostro Marx* ("Our Marx") and other writings of that same period. In his text *La rivoluzione contro il Capitale* he stated, for example, that Marx's perspective "was contaminated by positivist and naturalist incrustations".[1] Nonetheless, even if Marx had a questionable tendency to end up on positivistic ground (a tendency that Gramsci at the same time criticized and justified, as Marx, he said, is not a professional philosopher and "sometimes even he nods"[2]), his fundamental inspiration was radically different: for Gramsci, Marx, as to his valuable and important findings, can be placed in the grand theoretical line of philosophical idealism, represented in Germany by Hegel and in Italy by Croce.

---

1   AGR: 33 (SP1: 131).
2   HPC: 16–19 (NM: 348–351).

The criticisms Gramsci leveled at Marx – that in the fifties Togliatti deemed as "frankly incorrect"[3] – enabled nonetheless Gramsci to approach Marxism with intellectual freedom: it was unproductive, he thought, to fuel sterile arguments on what is or is not Marxism ("Marxists" and "Marxist" are terms that are "worn as thin as coins that have passed through too many hands")[4] and in any case, as he wrote in a famous passage, "Marx is not a Messiah who left a string of parables laden with categorical imperatives and absolute, unquestionable norms outside the categories of time and space".[5]

Gramsci's critique of the reduction of Marxism to a positivistic and deterministic doctrine, however, is not only the expression of a heightened cultural awareness, nourished by the best of the idealistic culture of the nineteenth and twentieth century; it is also directly linked to political aims. Lenin's revolution appeared as a hasty and utopist endeavor to the followers of evolutionary Marxism, for whom history *"non facit saltus"* ("does not make jumps") and the actualization of communism could only happen through the prior passage through the purgatory of capitalistic industrialization.

The criticism of the evolutionary corruption of historical materialism is not pure philosophical analysis; on the contrary, it is also a clear statement of the possibility and achievability of revolution. It is in considering the October Revolution that Gramsci grasps the weakness of historical materialism when reduced to an evolutionary schema. The Marxian doctrine, as Gramsci writes in an essay titled *Utopia*, teaches that, "political constitutions are necessarily dependent on economic structure, on forms of production and exchange".[6] If we take this statement in a mechanical way, then we can also maintain that, "Lenin is a utopian", and that, "the unfortunate Russian proletarians are prey to an utterly utopian illusion, so that a terrible awakening implacably awaits them".[7] But this is not the case, Gramsci writes, and the doctrine must be understood in a much more elaborate way.

> The unraveling of the causation is a complex and involved process [...]; history is not a mathematical calculation [...]. It is not the economic structure which directly determines political activity, but rather the way in which that structure and the so-called laws which govern its

---

3   Cf. Togliatti 1958.
4   AGR: 39 (SP1: 173).
5   AGR: 36 (SP1: 170).
6   AGR: 45 (SP1: 202).
7   Ibid.

development are interpreted. These laws have nothing in common with natural laws [...].[8]

Those who try to harness history in their preconceived schemas do not understand that history is a "free development – the birth and free integration of free energies –, which is quite different from natural evolution, just as man and human associations are different from molecules and molecular aggregates".[9] "Freedom is the inner force in history, exploding every pre-established schema".[10] Gramsci, in stating these points, finds himself very close to Croce.

He is indeed in good company when criticizing those who use historical materialism as a comprehensive explanatory schema. Engels had repeatedly insisted on this point, and his views had later been radicalized by Croce, who had claimed that the materialistic conception of history was neither a theory nor a reservoir of predictions; rather, it was only a guideline for historians to follow. Gramsci, however, did not only aim at understanding complicated historical processes in a more flexible way; he also aimed at assigning a greater importance to the role of free intellectual activity, to the men who act historically as "they *have a mind,* [...] they suffer, understand, rejoice, desire and reject".[11]

In the later development of his thought, Gramsci will reconsider this emphasis on the creative role of free intellectual activity. Nonetheless, he will keep himself faithful, over time, to some elements of this first encounter with Marx: the refusal of dogmatizing Marx's theories, the criticism of positivistic degenerations (perhaps, later, attributed more to the followers of Marx than to Marx himself), and the need to rethink historical materialism so as to overcome the subordination of intellectual work, and of the active and creative role of historical subjects, to economic and material forces.

2   Gramsci's Discussion of Marx in the Prison Notebooks: the Problem of Method

Although Marx is a constant reference all throughout Gramsci's body of work, it is in the *Quaderni del carcere* ("Prison Notebooks") that Gramsci's discussion of the German philosopher's thought is developed at its best. Before briefly

---

8   AGR: 45–46 (SP1: 203).
9   AGR: 50 (SP1: 207).
10   Ibid.
11   AGR: 45–46 (SP1.: 203).

retracing this discussion, we need however to focus our attention on the question of method, or, put more simply, on how Gramsci approaches, and thinks one should approach, Marx's texts. From this perspective, the enormous difference between Gramsci's approach and fideistic or dogmatic Marxism becomes immediately apparent.

Gramsci's awareness of the need of a historically and philologically rigorous method constitutes the first relevant difference between the two approaches. This awareness was constitutively part of Gramsci's intellectual formation, as he had a strong academic background (although he did not complete his degree).

> If one wishes to study the birth of a conception of the world which has never been systematically expounded by its founder, some preliminary detailed philological work has to be done. This has to be carried out with the most scrupulous accuracy, scientific honesty and intellectual loyalty and without any preconceptions, apriorism or *parti pris*.[12]

It makes no sense, for Gramsci, to approach Marx's writings without the utmost critical rigor: one must carefully distinguish between the works published by the author himself, those which remained unpublished, and "those which were published by a friend or disciple, but not without revisions, rewritings, cuts, etc., or in other words not without the active intervention of a publisher or editor. It is clear that the content of posthumous works has to be taken with great discretion and caution", as it cannot be excluded "the possibility that these works, particularly if they have been a long time in the making and if the author never decided to finish them, might have been repudiated or deemed unsatisfactory in whole or in part by the author".[13]

But this is not all. Besides the invitation, when reading Marx, to practice all the philological rigor required for approaching the works of a great thinker, Gramsci adds another fundamental methodological warning (which gets him closer to the approach that will be typical of the so-called "Western Marxism"): Marx and Engels cannot be considered as they were one and the same, because "the second is not the first". It is therefore problematic the fact that (since the end of the nineteenth century) "[Engels's] expositions, some of which are relatively systematic", for example the *Antidühring*, "have [...] been given a position

---

12   SPN: 382 (Q 16, § 2: 1840–1841).
13   SPN: 384 (Q 16, § 2: 1842).

in the front rank as an authentic source, and indeed as the only authentic source".[14]

There is also a second relevant aspect in the way Gramsci approaches Marxism: he highlights how a thought whose aim is to transform the consciousness and the way of thinking of the less cultured masses, easily ends up resorting to simplified formulas that betray its authentic content. This was true for the epigones of Marx, but also for Marx himself.

According to Gramsci, the metaphor according to which the economy constitutes the "anatomy" of civil society is ultimately misleading, but the use of this metaphor is justified by its ability to speak to those who would find philosophical language inaccessible. However, "the philosophy of praxis, in setting itself the task of the intellectual and moral reform of culturally backward social strata, has recourse to metaphors that at times are 'crude and violent' in their popularity",[15] and therefore one needs to interpret it without being misled by these rhetorically effective simplifications.

Simplifications of this kind can be found in Marx, but most of all in his epigones, who show a tendency to "mythicize" the theoretical contents elaborated by their master (a tendency also motivated by the need to invigorate combativeness and commitment):

> it should be noted how the deterministic, fatalistic and mechanistic element has been a direct ideological "aroma" emanating from the philosophy of praxis, rather like religion or drugs (in their stupefying effect). It has been made necessary and justified historically by the "subaltern" character of certain social strata [...]. Real will takes on the garments of an act of faith in a certain rationality of history and in a primitive and empirical form of impassioned finalism which appears in the role of a substitute for the Predestination or Providence of confessional religions.[16]

But we need to highlight a third aspect of the way Gramsci approaches Marx's works, also because this is a point on which many commentators still insist today: Gramsci's awareness of the fact that, in Marx, "theoretical and practical activity are indissolubly intertwined"[17] and that, for this reason, in reading his works one must take into account the contingent political commitment motivating them (or the "conjuncture", as today those who refer themselves to

---

14   SPN: 386 (Q 16, § 2: 1844).
15   FSPN: 315 (Q 11, § 50: 1474).
16   SPN: 336 (Q 11 § 12: 1388).
17   SPN: 383 (Q 16, § 2: 1841).

the thought of Althusser would say); Marx's writings cannot be understood as expressing some kind of absolute truth, valid *sub specie aeternitatis*.

Gramsci's considerations about Marx, in my opinion, can also be applied to Gramsci himself: for him, too, society can be transformed through organized political and intellectual activity in a determined historical phase. This, of course, also has repercussions on the way he addresses the major questions in Marx's thought, in particular those concerning historical materialism. The close connection between thought and political action, between theory and practice, is a double-edged sword: on the one hand, it prevents intellectual activity from falling into academicism and sterility, on the other, however, threatens to bend it towards the urgencies and priorities of politics, thereby diverting it from the dispassionate rigor necessary for guiding action in a lucid way.

3   Historical Materialism according to Gramsci (and Croce)

In order to further elaborate on the contents of Gramsci's interpretation of Marx and to point out some of its most relevant elements, I think we should first of all compare it with the one proposed by Croce. Croce's reading of Marx is one of the two conflicting views (the other one is Bukharin's) that Gramsci considers in the *Quaderni del carcere* ("Prison Notebooks").

The main interpretive points that Croce outlines in the essays he wrote at end of the century[18] (which Gramsci almost counterposes to the later ones) are the following:

a)   historical materialism has nothing to do with "metaphysical" materialism;
b)   Marxism is not a philosophy of history – this had been the topic of the first friendly debate between Croce and Gentile;
c)   historical materialism must be understood as nothing more than a fruitful paradigm for interpreting history;
d)   the theory of exploitation does not make sense from a purely economic point of view (it makes sense only from a different perspective), and the socialist option does not necessarily follow from the Marxist analysis of society.

Here we will leave aside a further point, that is, the critique by Croce, that Gramsci disputed, of the tendency of the rate of profit to fall.

Gramsci's interpretation of Marx, on a particular point, resonates with the one proposed by Croce: he, too, radically separates Marx's historical materialism from metaphysical materialism. Gramsci also shares one of Croce's

---

18   Cf. Croce 2001. Cf. also Tuozzolo 2008.

justifications for this stance by referring to F.A. Lange's *History of Materialism*, which rightly, as Croce had claimed, did not mention the philosophy of Marx.[19] Always very harsh, moreover, is Gramsci's critique against the reductions of Marx's thought to the old materialism, in particular the French one,[20] as those attempted by Plekhanov and Bukharin.

What to say on the theoretical status of historical materialism and the problems that, on this topic, had already arisen by the end of the nineteenth century? How should we understand Marx's words according to which "the mode of production in material life determines (*bedingt*) the general character of the social, political, and spiritual processes of life"?[21]

As is well known, Engels had tried, in some of his letters, to better clarify the fundaments of historical materialism, and to dispute its deterministic and simplistic readings. Croce, in turn, radicalized Engel's definition (who had stated that historical materialism is first of all "a guideline for study"),[22] thereby reducing Marx's theory to a canon for interpreting history. And Gramsci?

Gramsci, first of all, highlights Engel's famous statement according to which the economic base is only *"in the last instance* the determining moment in history"[23] and agrees with him in maintaining that, although the structure retains its primacy, the superstructure acts, in turn, on the base.

In relation to Croce, Gramsci's position is more complex. He does not argue frontally with Croce, who had substantially de-theoreticized historical materialism by turning it into a mere guideline for historians. He just observes that Croce arrives to this idea of the "canon of interpretation" by means of exclusion (if historical materialism is not this nor that, then what is it?) and without, furthermore, demonstrating his thesis in a conclusive way. The Croce of this

---

19   SPN: 456 (Q 11, § 16: 1410).

20   SPN: 162 (Q 13, § 18: 1592).

21   Marx 1913: 11.

22   "Unsere Geschichtsauffassung aber ist vor allem eine Anleitung beim Studium, kein Hebel der Konstruktion à la Hegelianertum" (*Letter to Conrad Schmidt*, August 5th, 1890).

23   "Nach materialistischer Geschichtsauffassung ist das in letzter Instanz bestimmende Moment in der Geschichte die Produktion und Reproduktion des wirklichen Lebens. Mehr hat weder Marx noch ich je behauptet. Wenn nun jemand das dahin verdreht, das ökonomische Moment sei das einzig bestimmende, so verwandelt er jenen Satz in eine nichtssagende, abstrakte, absurde Phrase" (*Letter to J. Bloch*, September 21st, 1890). In the analysis that he devotes to the structure-superstructure problem, Giuseppe Cospito observes that, in reconsidering the Engelsian issue of the "last instance", Gramsci gradually tends to radicalize it. In the *Quaderni del carcere* ("Prison Notebooks"), a first formulation in which Gramsci writes that according to Engels "the economy is 'in the last instance' the motor of history" is rewritten as "the economy is *only* in the 'last instance' the incentive of history" (my italics); cf. Cospito 2004: 227–246, 242.

phase, Gramsci writes, is problematic and "cautious", very different from how he will be when discussing Marx's works in later writings. Moreover, in a sarcastic but fairly sympathetic way, Gramsci overturns the idea of the interpretive canon against Croce himself: first of all, he gives Croce the credit for having "drawn attention to the study of the factors of culture and ideas as elements of political domination, to the function of the great intellectuals in state life, to the moment of hegemony and consent as the necessary form of the concrete historical bloc".[24] After having sung him high praise, however, Gramsci turns against Croce the idea of the "canon", as he writes that, for the philosophy of praxis, the ethical-political conception of history is "one of the canons of historical interpretation that must always be borne in mind in the study and detailed analysis of history as it unfolds, if the intention is to construct an integral history rather than partial or extrinsic histories".[25]

Hence, just as the first Croce gave credit to Marx for having highlighted the economic moment, so Gramsci gives credit to Croce for having emphasized the ethical-political and spiritual moment. To the later Croce, who according to Gramsci had changed almost all his previous stances, the latter directs instead a harsh critique: of having attributed to Marx, in order to demolish him, a thesis that did not belong at all to the author of the *Manifesto*, namely that superstructures would be "mere appearances and illusions". This thesis was absolutely extraneous to the young Croce, as well as being, from Gramsci's point of view, totally erroneous – since, for the latter, superstructures are an "objective and operating" reality. And such they were, according to Gramsci, also for Marx; because it is through them – and here Gramsci broadens to the extreme the meaning of a famous passage of the *Vorwort* ("Preface") of 1859 to *Zur Kritik der politischen Öknomie* ("A Contribution to the Critique of Political Economy") – that individuals and classes "become conscious of their own social being, their own strength, their own tasks, their own becoming".[26]

Leaving aside, however, the emphatic anti-Marxist polemics characterizing, among Croce's writings, the ones chronologically closer to the *Quaderni del carcere* ("Prison Notebooks"), we can say that Gramsci's and Croce's perspectives are not so distant from each other; Gramsci himself goes to show this, when he observes that the philosophy of praxis does not rule out an "ethico-political history" at all, since it accords great importance to the moment of hegemony and of cultural and moral leadership.[27]

---

24   FSPN: 332 (Q 10I: 1211).
25   Ibid.
26   FSPN: 548 (Q10II, § 41: 1319).
27   FSPN: 493–494 (Q 10I, § 7: 1224–1225).

In conclusion, what of the debate on historical materialism? What can we say, in the last instance (to paraphrase Engels), on the discussion concerning the relation between structure and superstructure, which by Gramsci (and not only by him) was seen as the crucial problem of historical materialism?[28]

If Engels claims the primacy of the structure, but with all possible corrections and retroactions, and Croce maintains the primacy of the superstructure, but with the acknowledgment that materialism also has a point, what is Gramsci's stance? With the premise that he always saw his considerations on this theme as a work in progress, and even doubted to be able to arrive at a univocal solution,[29] we can try to draw some conclusions on this topic.

Differently from systemic or Hegelian theories, that interpret society as a connection of circularly integrated functions, without hierarchical subordinations (also Lukács will move in this direction when claiming, in *Geschichte und Klassenbewußtsein* – "History and Class Consciousness"–, that the defining feature of Marxism is its notion of social totality), historical materialism subscribes to an asymmetric vision of the social whole: from the synchronic point of view, the sphere of production *conditions* the other spheres more than it is itself conditioned by them; from the diachronic point of view, the sphere of production transforms itself for endogenous reasons, while the other spheres are transformed by it, instead of being generated through (as Gramsci himself writes) "parthenogenesis". Historical materialism stands or falls with these two theses. Does Gramsci rethink or even reject them in the last phase of his theoretical itinerary? I do not believe that this question can be answered in a totally univocal way. On the one hand, in many of his formulations, Gramsci holds firm on the "classic" idea of a primacy of the structure. On the other hand, however, he distances himself from this classic thesis and progressively leaves it behind, the more he develops and refines his original perspective. As Cospito writes, Gramsci on the one side tends to "question the identification of the structure with the economy, by speaking of 'politico-economic structure'[30] or 'cultural-economic structure'",[31] or by considering "the priority of the politico-economic fact – that is, the 'structure' – as a point of reference and as a non-mechanical dialectical 'causation' of the superstructures".[32]

On the other hand, in Gramsci's writings, there are many expressions that can lead one to think, especially for what concerns the last phase of the

---

28 Cf. SPN: 365–366 (Q 1011, § 12: 1249–1250).

29 Gerratana 1975: XXVI.

30 SPN: 93 (Q 19, § 26: 2037).

31 Cospito 2009: 821.

32 PN2: 231 (Q 4, § 56: 503).

philosopher's theoretical itinerary, that in the end he completely rejected the architectonic metaphor[33] characterizing historical materialism and its idea of a hierarchy of spheres. For example, he writes that, speaking in terms of "historical bloc", "the material forces are the content and ideologies are the form. This distinction between form and content is just heuristic, because material forces would be historically inconceivable without form and ideologies would be individual fantasies without material forces".[34] In conclusion, Gramsci seems sometimes to assert a symmetric and reciprocal relation between structure and superstructure,[35] but, at the same time, we cannot rule out from his theoretical horizon two other possibilities: the persistence of a certain primacy of the economic base, on the one hand, and, within the context of this primacy, its redefinition in the terms of a "political-economic structure", on the other.

Bibliography

Gramsci's Works and Abbreviations

AGR: Forgacs, D. (ed.) (2000), *The Gramsci Reader. Selected Writings 1916–1935* (New York: NYU Press).

FSPN: Boothman, D. (ed.) (1995), *Further Selections from the Prison Notebooks* (Minneapolis: Minnesota University Press).

HPC: Cavalcanti, P., Piccone, P. (eds.) (1975), *History, Philosophy and Culture in the Young Gramsci* (St. Louis: Telos Press).

NM: Caprioglio, S. (ed.) (1984), *Il nostro Marx (1918–1919)* (Torino: Einaudi).

PN: Buttigieg, J.A. (ed.) (1992, 1996, 2007), *Prison Notebooks* (New York: Columbia University Press), 3 vols.

Q: Gerratana, V. (ed.) (1975), *Quaderni del carcere* (Torino: Einaudi), 4 vols.

SPI: Spriano, P. (ed.), (1973), *Scritti politici* (Roma: Editori Riuniti), 3 vols.

SPN: Hoare, Q., Nowell-Smith, G. (eds.) (1971), *Selection from the Prison Notebooks* (New York: International Publishers).

Other Works

Cospito, G. (2004), *Struttura-superstruttura*, in Frosini, F., Liguori, G. (eds.), *Le parole di Gramsci* (Roma: Carocci).

---

33   Cf. Cospito 2004: 235.

34   PN3: 172 (Q 7, § 21: 869).

35   PN3: 340 (Q 8, § 182: 1051). Cf. also Voza 2009, Cospito 2009.

Cospito, G. (2009), *Struttura*, in Liguori, G., Voza, P. (eds.), *Dizionario gramsciano 1926–1937* (Roma: Carocci).

Croce, B. (2001), Materialismo storico ed economia marxistica, in Rascaglia, M., Zoppi, S. (eds.), *Materialismo storico ed economia marxistica* (Napoli: Bibliopolis).

Gerratana, V. (1975), Prefazione, in *Quaderni del carcere* (Torino: Einaudi), I vol.

Marx, K. (1913), *A Contribution to the Critique of Political Economy* (Chicago: Charles H. Kerr and Company).

Togliatti, P. [1958] (1979), *Gramsci and Leninism*, in Sassoon, D. (ed.), *On Gramsci and Other Writings* (London: Lawrence & Wishart).

Tuozzolo, C. (2008), *"Marx possibile". Benedetto Croce teorico marxista 1869–1897* (Milano: Franco Angeli).

Voza, P. (2009), *Blocco storico*, in Liguori, G., Voza, P. (eds.), *Dizionario gramsciano 1926–1937* (Roma: Carocci).

CHAPTER 7

Gramsci, the October Revolution and Its "Translation" in the West

Guido Liguori

1 From Sardinia to Torino

To understand the way in which Antonio Gramsci related to the two Russian revolutions of 1917, and in particular to the October Revolution, it is necessary to keep in mind his very particular upbringing.

Already in Sardinia, Gramsci had started to read socialist newspapers and pamphlets (above all thanks to the influence of his older brother Gennaro, who was one of the directors of the workers' union in Cagliari), books and articles written by the revolutionary Georges Sorel (that influenced him deeply), by people, like Salvemini, who belonged to the Left (even if he would soon leave the Socialist Party) and by Antonio Labriola (the first real Italian Marxist).

From the years of his youth in Sardinia, Gramsci was also influenced, perhaps above all, by the bourgeois culture (opposition to Giolitti and his ideas), which was the particular field where he was formed. The so-called "Florentine magazines" like "Il Leonardo" and "La Voce" of Papini and Prezzolini, philosophies such as neo-idealism, pragmatism, and that of Bergson made up a culture that was almost completely focused on the re-evaluation of the "subject" against that which had been the dominant philosophy of the second half of the 1800s and had notably influenced even Marxism and the workers' movement, with its idea of "objectivism" (epistemological, historical and political): a vision that still deeply influenced the main currents of the workers' movement at the beginning of the 1900s.

In 1911, Gramsci moved to Torino to begin his studies at the Faculty of Literature and Philosophy, thanks to a scholarship that was just enough to survive on.[1] Even before the Great War, he joined the socialist party in Torino. His Marxism at this time was very particular: because of his cultural formation, the Marxism of the young Gramsci was against the trend of the time. His Marxism was subjectivistic, anti-deterministic, anti-economistic, influenced by neo-idealism and the philosophy of Bergson, mediated in part by Sorel. It

---

1 Cf. Gramsci 1994: 138, Gramsci to Carlo, September 12th, 1927 (LC2: 117).

was an original but also *immature Marxism*, centered on (in more than one passage) the absolute and idealistic supremacy of the will.

In these years, there was no scarcity of important writings with an anti-deterministic vision, even concerning revolutionary processes. In his 1916 article, *Socialismo e cultura* ("Socialism and culture") for example, he put forward a definition of culture as the conquest and valuing of one's own self and thus a growth of his own subjectivity.[2] It underlined the importance of awareness and of ideas in the processes of change, in the great revolutions. Gramsci writes:

> every revolution has been preceded by an intense labour of criticism, by the diffusion of culture and the spread of ideas [...] The latest example, the closest to us and hence least foreign to our own time, is that of the French Revolution. The preceding cultural period, called the Enlightenment [...] was a magnificent revolution in itself.[3]

This anti-deterministic subjectivism melded with another closely connected element: the importance of the will, that was also the desire to participate, fleeing from passivity. It is the famous "I hate the indifferent",[4] the cry hurled out by Gramsci in January 1917, just a few weeks before the February Revolution in Russia.

2   The Russian Revolution

Starting from the first comments of the February Revolution, Gramsci read the events in Russia as the revenge of the socialists who had not betrayed the spirit of the International and who saw a "proletarian revolution"[5] in the events of Petrograd.

He was not completely wrong, as at the beginning of the "first revolution" of 1917, the February Revolution, there had been a workers' demonstration in Petrograd as well as the women's demonstration on March 8th, a day which corresponded with February 24th in the Julian calendar that was then used in Russia (14 days behind the Gregorian calendar, used in the West); and, also, the

---

2   Cf. AGR: 58 (Gramsci 2016: 57).
3   Ibid.
4   HPC: 64–66 (Gramsci 2016: 73 ff.)
5   SPW-1: 28 (Gramsci 2017: 34).

switching of many soldiers to the side of the insurgents (armed peasants) who instead of shooting rioters, fired at the Tsarist police.

What were the background characteristics of the event, for Gramsci? The "Russian revolution" for him had "been innocent of Jacobinism", that is, it "did not have to crush the majority of the people by the use of violence".[6] (It is notable that until 1921 – when his opinion changed on the basis of the work of the French historian Albert Mathiez, that positively underlines the similarities between Jacobins and Bolsheviks[7] – Gramsci, influenced by Sorel, and ignoring Lenin and even Marx, was decidedly anti-Jacobin).

For Gramsci, Jacobinism and the Jacobin revolution, were at that time (in 1917), a bourgeois phenomenon: of a minority that "served particular interests, the interest of its own class".[8] On the other hand, the "Russian revolutionaries" did not want to substitute one dictatorship for another and – he claimed – they would have had, through universal suffrage, the support of a huge part of the "Russian proletariat", if only they could have expressed themselves freely.

It was a vision that we could say was *naïve* in terms of the revolutionary process, both for that concerning events in Russia – where the revolutionary forces were in reality much more internally composite and divided than Gramsci knew and understood at first –, and in the conviction that universal suffrage was enough to guarantee the rise of the true will of the proletariat.

Here, Gramsci disregards – contrary to what he would do with great acuity in his mature writings from prison, but also, partly, in the *"Consigli di fabbica"* (factory workers' councils) period of the journal "L'Ordine Nuovo" ("The New Order") and the "biennio rosso" ("Two Red Years") – the prerequisites of democracy, from the basically egalitarian elements (in terms of culture, information, awareness, freedom from need) that an electoral body should possess to express themselves without "self-serving ends".

After a few months, the young socialist will begin the analysis of the internal distinctions within the great revolutionary event that had archived Tsarist power, but not the war.

Gramsci's attention was moving, though not without some understandable oscillation given the scarcity of information, towards the Bolshevik component (a term that was then translated in Italy as "Maximalist", a category of the Italian political panorama of the time), identified as the force that did not accept that the revolution would stop at its bourgeois-democratic stage, and expected it to continue until the conquest of a socialist society instead: "Lenin

---

6 Ibid.
7 Cf. Medici 2004: 113 ff.
8 SPW-1: 28 (Gramsci 2017: 35).

[...] and his Bolshevik comrades – he wrote – are convinced that socialism can be achieved at any time. They are nourished on Marxist thought. They are revolutionaries, not evolutionists".[9]

Here the polemic is evident against the evolutionism of Kautsky and the Second International (social-democratic and reformist) represented in Italy by the moderate socialism of people like Treves and Turati, in the name of that revolutionary subjectivism that distinguished Gramsci during this period: in Russia – he added – "the revolution continues", so that men, all men can be "the creators of their destiny".

3   Kerensky and Lenin

In the meantime, even before the October Revolution, the enthusiasm for what had happened in Russia was spreading across Italy and the rest of Europe. The defeat of Caporetto (which took place in the same days as the capture of the Winter Palace, between October 24th and November 9th) was just around the corner, also caused by an increasing amount of criticism against the war and the inhuman method – that of Cadorna and the other officials on either side of the trenches – of using soldiers as meat to be slaughtered, with an ease that also stemmed from a deep-rooted classist attitude.

This same impetus was one of the main causes of the revolution in Russia, perhaps even the principle one. It is not surprising then, that "do as they do in Russia" began to be the password that circulated among the popular and subaltern classes of a large part of Europe, where the name of "Lenin" was beginning to be largely known and praised.

And Gramsci was no different: the choice is between Kerensky and Lenin, he wrote in August,[10] that is, between the new head of the Russian Provisional Government formed on August 6th, and the revolutionary leader now being hunted by the new government's police and being forced to take refuge in Finland. There he writes Государство и революция ("The State and Revolution") in a few weeks until the moment when he must interrupt the draft to enable his return to Russia to lead the revolution (instead of just theorizing it).

More than a month before the October Revolution, Gramsci warned that the time was near to decide between liberal revolution and socialist revolution, measuring "what is the effective force of the socialist revolutionaries and

---

9   SPW-1: 32 (Gramsci 2017: 39).
10   Cf. Gramsci 2017: 44 ff.

what is that of the bourgeois revolutionaries".[11] Gaining freedom (from the Tsarist autocracy), the revolution, for Gramsci, should continue forward, reaching "final goals": socialism, "the freedom to begin the concrete transformation of the economic and social world of the old Tsarist Russia. The compromise with the bourgeoisie is no longer useful, it is no longer necessary, it is an obstacle".[12]

4   A Revolution against "Capital"

Between October 24th and 25th according to the Russian calendar (between November 7th and 8th in the Western calendar), the Winter Palace was occupied and the Soviets (hegemonized by the Bolsheviks) took power.

Gramsci's comment written at the end of November is famous. For the Sardinian socialist, it was a "revolution against *Capital*": Marx's book, against those who had given that book and Marxism an economistic and deterministic reading that was "stadial", in which no socialist revolution would have been possible in backwards Russia before an adequate development of the "capitalist stage" of industry and therefore of the Russian working class. Now – wrote Gramsci – "these maximalists have seized power and established their dictatorship, and are creating the socialist framework within which the revolution will have to settle down".[13]

The Marxism of the Bolsheviks was "constructed" by Gramsci in the image and semblance of his ideas: a historicist Marxism, derived from Hegel and freed from the slag of positivism. Once again, the will triumphs in Gramsci's vision: associated human beings can understand "economic facts, judging them and adapting them to their will until this becomes the driving force of the economy and moulds objective reality, which lives and moves and comes to resemble a current of volcanic lava that can be channeled wherever and in whatever way the will determines".[14]

More than its provocative beginning (the "revolution against *Capital*" of Marx), in reality, the article captured one of the deep motivations of the October Revolution: war had made an unprecedented and unexpected event possible. Marx had "foreseen the foreseeable", stated the young socialist revolutionary journalist (then only 26 years old), but he could not have foreseen the

---

11   Gramsci 2017: 46.
12   Gramsci 2017: 47.
13   AGR: 32–33 (Gramsci 2017: 50).
14   AGR: 33 (Gramsci 2017: 51).

First World War and its unprecedented character, which "would have aroused the will of the popular collective in Russia" much faster than normal ("this is why, *under normal conditions* – Gramsci added – the canons of Marxist historical criticism grasp reality"[15]). He continues: "in Russia the war galvanized the people's will. As a result of the sufferings accumulated over three years, their will became as one almost overnight. Famine was imminent, and hunger, death from hunger, could claim anyone, could crush tens of millions of men at one stroke. Mechanically at first, then actively and consciously agter the first revolution, the people's will became as one".[16]

Today we can affirm that Russia went through its revolution because Lenin had known how to read the "conjuncture". He had known how to make "a concrete analysis of the concrete situation" (to quote a famous Leninist motto). Historical events are always *individual*, politics and history are, for Lenin and Gramsci, *idiographic* disciplines: every generalization is a mistake.

5   A Field of Possibilities

The more mature Gramsci would reformulate his vision of the revolutionary process, arriving at defining it as a relationship of reciprocal influence and equilibrium between "relationships of force" and revolutionary initiative. From the October Revolution onwards, in fact, in Gramsci's writing there begins to be reasoning and considerations that are more coherent with the Marxist tradition. Gramsci's Marxism starts to free itself from its idealistic incrustations. In the article, *Il nostro Marx* ("Our Marx"), published May 4th, 1918, on the eve of the centenary of the birth of the German revolutionary, he states that before Marx, "history was only the domain of ideas" while "with Marx, history continues to be the domain of the ideas, the spirit, and of the conscious activity of single or associated individuals". But, continues Gramsci, thanks to Marx, "the ideas and the spirit substantiate themselves, losing their arbitrariness" and "their substance is in economy, in practical activity, in the systems and relationships of production and exchange". For this reason, "an idea realizes itself [...] in that it finds the justification and the way to establish itself in economic reality". It follows that, in order to know "what the historical ends of a country, a society" one must "know first of all what systems and relations of production and exchange obtain in that country, that society".[17]

---

15   AGR: 34 (Gramsci 2017: 51).
16   Ibid.
17   AGR: 37–38 (Gramsci 2016: 132–133).

The vision of the more mature Gramsci will not lose the importance given to will and subjectivity, but the historical-social reality in the *Quaderni del carcere* ("Prison Notebooks") will be a *field of possibilities*, that the objective conditions offer to the subject within which will be determined a certain outcome rather than another depending on the action and the capabilities of the subject himself.

Gramsci's youthful hyper-subjectivism will be surpassed starting from the new situation that the October Revolution had created and that also repositioned his vision on a new and more concrete terrain.

It was precisely from Gramsci's adherence to the international political movement that was born with the "second Russian revolution", that his Marxism began to free itself from the idealistic and spiritual incrustations that had strongly conditioned him in the previous period.

6   A New Conception of the World

In the following years, Gramsci passes through difficult and crucial experiences. First of all, the "biennio rosso" 1919–1920 ("Two Red Years") when he became one of the most unique and important representatives of the *"consigli di fabbrica"* (factory workers' councils) thought in Europe, taking on the leadership of the movement of the factory councils in Turin and developing an original concept of self-government for the working classes that was original and also different from the soviet model in Russia.

The failure of the workers' movement in Turin, however, opened his eyes to the complexity and variety of the Italian situation, to the fact that not all of Italy was like Turin – a modern industrial society, standardized and characterized by the "sturdy fortresses and emplacements"[18] of "civil society", as Gramsci expressed in the *Quaderni del carcere* ("Prison Notebooks"); but also on the limits of Italian socialist party that was revolutionary in word but immobile and confused in reality.

The failure of the workers' and socialist movement of the "Two Red Years" also gave birth to the dramatic phase of the Fascist reaction and the historical defeat suffered by the workers' movement in Italy. These events provoked a deep rethinking by Gramsci and induced him to accept Lenin's teaching on the conditions of the possibility of a revolution in the West, above all thanks to his stay in the Soviet capital from June of 1922 until the end of 1923.

---

18   PN3: 169 (Q 7, § 17: 866).

The lesson that came from Lenin was that of a crisis of capitalism that would not necessarily immediately turn into a wave of revolution. It was under Lenin's influence that Gramsci developed the conviction that the West could not "do like in Russia" because in the West the "political superstructures" created by the development of capitalism and by mass society made every possible revolutionary strategy slower and more complex. Already in 1924, Gramsci had developed *in nuce* some of the themes that would be those central to the *Quaderni del carcere*[19]. The revolution of 1917 needed to be *translated* into the specific situation of developed capitalistic societies.

Gramsci therefore arrives at a complete rethinking of his youthful theoretical baggage. In mature Gramsci, the revolutionary will go side by side with the most objective knowledge of the situation: a precise social and historical analysis of the field on which the struggle plays out. Gramsci in prison, arrives at destroying the morphological difference between East and West, and consequently between war of movement and war of position,[20] and comes to the conclusion that the Russian Revolution had been the last 18th century-style revolution, the last insurrection-revolution, at least in Europe or in the developed world.[21] In the West, the modern structure of mass society, the new interpenetration between state and civil society, the weight and importance of the mechanisms of the formation of consensus are all factors that bring Gramsci to a real *revolution of the concept of revolution*, not only regarding the subjectivistic and idealistic vision of his youthful period, but also regarding the *classic* and sometimes stereotyped conception of the Marxist and Leninist tradition. It is not (as is sometimes argued) because Gramsci emerges from Marxism or from the revolutionary tradition, with a classically reformist approach. The will for change does not lose its anchoring in social class, its heart in the economic world and in social relationships, but sees all the complexity of modern political action. It refutes economic conceptions based on the relation between economic crisis and revolution; it identifies as fundamental the public and private structures that form a widespread common sense, and considers it essential to launch the challenge of conquering the general consensus. In other words, it underlines the importance of a cultural and ideological reflection that could offer a new conception of the world and could form a new common sense of the people.

---

19   Cf. Liguori 2015: 249.
20   As regards the main Gramscian categories to which reference is made here cf. Liguori, Voza 2009.
21   Cf. PN3: 148 (Q 6, § 208: 845).

It is a conception that, by highlighting the decisive importance of consensus, cultural reflection and widespread common sense, lays the foundation for a *democratic* political struggle that is compatible with the strategy of the conquest of hegemony.

Bibliography

Gramsci's Works and Abbreviations

Gramsci, A. (2016), *Masse e partito. Antologia 1910–1926, G. Liguori (ed.)* (Roma: Editori Riuniti).

Gramsci, A. (2017), *Come alla volontà piace. Scritti sulla Rivoluzione russa*, Liguori, G. (ed.) (Roma: Castelvecchi).

AGR: Forgacs, D. (ed.) (2000), *The Gramsci Reader. Selected Writings 1916–1935* (New York: NYU Press).

HPC: Cavalcanti, P., Piccone, P. (eds.) (1975), *History, Philosophy and Culture in the Young Gramsci* (St. Louis: Telos Press).

LC2: Santucci, A. (ed.) (1996), *Lettere dal carcere. 1926–1937* (Palermo: Sellerio).

PN: Buttigieg, J.A. (ed.) (1992, 1996, 2007), *Prison Notebooks* (New York: Columbia University Press), 3 vols.

Q: Gerratana, V. (ed.) (1975), *Quaderni del carcere* (Torino: Einaudi), 4 vols.

SPW-1: Hoare, Q., Nowell Smith, G. (eds.) (1977), *Selections from Political Writings, 1910–1920* (London: Lawrence & Wishart; New York: International Publisher).

Other Works

Liguori, G. (2015), *Teoria e politica nel marxismo di Antonio Gramsci*, in Petrucciani, S. (ed.), *Storia del marxismo*, vol. 1, *Socialdemocrazia, revisionismo, rivoluzione* (Roma: Carocci).

Liguori, G., Voza, P. (eds.) (2009), *Dizionario gramsciano 1926–1937* (Roma: Carocci).

Medici, R. (2004), *Giacobinismo*, in Frosini, F., Liguori, G. (eds.), *Le parole di Gramsci* (Roma: Carocci).

CHAPTER 8

On the Transition to Communism

Alberto Burgio

1   Between the Past and the Future

The question of the transition to Communism – in particular, the problem of the *structure* of the process, given that on its chronological placement Gramsci in the *Quaderni del carcere* ("Prison Notebooks") does not venture to forecast what concerns Western Europe and Italy – is the subject of several notes in the *Quaderni* as well some other important texts written before his imprisonment. As always with Gramsci, one must see whether the texts can be organized into a coherent collection identifiable as a theory.

First, one must consider that this question shapes a specific case within the framework of the general discourse on historical transitions, discourse that Gramsci – as in general in revolutionary Marxism – conducts mostly along the lines of the schema outlined by Marx in the *Vorwort* ("Preface") of 1859. As it is known, the *Quaderni del carcere* refers to the text of the *Vorwort* several times, emphasizing its theoretical relevance (it contains fundamental "principles of historical methodology"[1]) and developing the schema by integrating it with a theory of periodization based on the polarity "lasting"/"constituting an epoch".[2]

But this schema does not fully exhaust Marx's reflection on transitions. In Marx there is also a specific theory of transition (and of revolution) that does not consider the past, but the future (or, in the case of the Commune of Paris, the present): not the transitions to feudalism and capitalism, but the end of bourgeois modernity and the coming of the "new society" liberated from the exploitation of man by man. In this regard, several works of Marx – all well known to Gramsci – demonstrate a different model (actually, the opposite model) with respects to that contemplated in the *Vorwort* of 1859. Already in the *Manifest* (and little by little in *Die Klassenkämpfe in Frankreich 1848 bis 1850* – "The Class Struggles in France, 1848 to 1850" –, *Der Bürgerkrieg in*

---

1   SPN: 432 (Q 11 § 22: 1422).
2   Cf. Burgio 2018: 434–8; on Gramsci's idea of "constituting an epoch", cf. Burgio 2014: Ch. 5; on the role of Marx's *Vorwort* in the complete view of Gramsci's prison reflections, cf. Burgio 2003: 65–69. See these works also for other bibliographical references.

Frankreich – "The Civil War in France" – and *Kritik des Gothaer Programms* – "Critique of the Gotha Program") the sequence of process > event is overturned, in the way that Marx imagines political events which open the road to the process of construction in the new social formation, a process which involves "a period of political transition" where the command of the new state is exercised as "*the revolutionary dictatorship of the proletariat*".[3]

2   The Norm and the Exception

When Gramsci is reasoning like a critical historian of modernization, he uses the schema of Marx's *Vorwort* ("Preface"), while when he reflects on the political urgency of the workers' revolution (in other words, on the need to *anticipate* the sequence of processes *accelerating* the times) he instead uses these other works by Marx. And, besides that, it goes without saying that he uses the theoretical (and *in primis* practical) contribution by Lenin.

A universally known, and often fundamentally misunderstood, text from the pre-prison period is the article that Grasmci published (first in "Avanti!" on December 24, 1917, and then in "Grido del Popolo" on January 5, 1918) with the title *La rivoluzione contro il "Capitale"* ("The Revolution Against the 'Capital'"). In this article he celebrates the "Bolshevik revolution" and the establishment of a "dictatorship", necessary for the developing of "the socialist framework within which the revolution will have to settle down if it is to continue to develop harmoniously".[4] It is important to notice the emphasis placed here by Gramsci on the *anomaly* (with respect to the general schema of transitions) represented by the October Revolution. If, "*under normal conditions* the two classes of the capitalist world create history through an ever more intensified class struggle",[5] in Russia the intertwining of the revolution with the World War upset the situation. On the background of unspeakable suffering provoked by war and famine, "the socialist propaganda forged the will of the Russian people" that now – denying both the Mensheviks and the evolved "Marxists" theories – was about to burn the stages of history (Gramsci speaks of "immediate socialism") *generating* "the conditions needed for the total achievement of their [the revolutionaries'] goal".[6]

---

3   MEW 19: 28. Cf. MEW 4: 481; MEW 7: 89; MEW 17: 338–339, 342, 349.
4   SPW-1: 34 (Gramsci 1982: 513).
5   SPW-1: 35 (Gramsci 1982: 514).
6   SPW-1: 36 (Gramsci 1982: 515–516).

Naturally, *La rivoluzione contro il "Capitale"* was not the only pre-prison text to deal with the structure of the revolutionary process. Gramsci returns to the subject in two important articles in particular that appeared within two months of each other in "Ordine Nuovo" in the summer of 1920. In these articles he defines the "political power" of the working class as "the defensive organization and condition of development for a given order in the relations of production and distribution of wealth"[7] (*Due rivoluzioni* – "Two Revolutions") and reiterates that the working class "will achieve its liberation only by passing through a period of 'dictatorship', a period of restrictions, a period characterized as a workers' State"[8] (*Che cosa intendiamo per "demagogia"?* – "What do we mean by 'demagogy'?").

And the mature Gramsci? The Gramsci of the *Quaderni* ("Prison Notebooks")? Fashionable today is a vulgar revisionism that aims to rip Gramsci – especially the imprisoned Gramsci – from the damaged history of 20th century Communism in order to preserve him in the pantheon of the polite and palatable "classics". A crucial junction in this operation is the pseudo-philology at the service of the Italian national edition, poised to dismember the body of the *Prison Notebooks* in order to inhibit an organic reading; to shatter it by dramatizing the question of internal chronology beyond reason (it is strange that the work of an inmate segregated from the world can no longer be spoken of as a unified text). But the question of the transition to communism is one that is not easily tamed. This question is also, for the connections that link it to the living history of the 20th century (before than to the texts of the top theorists of revolutionary Marxism), one that ridicules any attempt to pass off the sweetened image of Gramsci the "good democrat".

The *Prison Notebooks* deliver a *rigorous Leninist theory of the transition to communism*, connected (as is easy to understand) by a series of annotations in which Gramsci expresses passionately favorable judgments towards the revolutionary experience in progress in the Soviet Union. Let's consider – with the necessary speed – at least the principal texts of this theoretical and political constellation.

3   The Construction of "Regulated Society"

The § 88 of *Quaderno 6* ("Notebook 6") contains a key passage with regards to regulated society. The following is how Gramsci succinctly describes the

---

7 SPW-1: 305 (Gramsci 1987: 569–570).
8 SPW-1: 323 (Gramsci 1987: 643).

process that (after the conquest of political power by the working class) leads
to the construction of a society free from rule:

> It is possible to imagine the state-coercion element withering away grad-
> ually, as the increasingly conspicuous elements of regulated society (or
> ethical state or civil society) assert themselves. [...] In the theory of state ➤
> regulated society (from a phase in which state equals government to
> a phase in which state is identified with civil society), there must be a
> transition phase of state as night watchman, that is, of a coercive organi-
> zation that will protect the development of those elements of regulated
> society that are continually on the rise and, precisely because they are on
> the rise, will gradually reduce the state's authoritarian and coercive in-
> terventions. This is not to say that one should think of a new "liberalism",
> even if the beginning of an era of organic freedom were at hand.[9]

The dynamic described consists of the gradual *transformation* of the State
into an organism that is increasingly free from constrictive elements (institutions and practices), until its *resolution* in the collection of social-economic
relationships and administrative functions: until its complete metamorphosis
into a "regulated society", center of self-government and of "organic freedom"
(non-individualistic, but collective and common); until its "gradual reduction"
(until its extinguishing) as a coercive apparatus above the social field (which
is why Gramsci speaks, shortly before, of the realization of a "state without a
state").[10]

   This, in short, is the heart of the argument. There are two remaining problems to resolve, however. One must understand, in this schema, what is meant
by the expressions "coercive state" and "night-watchman state". One must also
identify the starting point of this process with certainty.

   Let's begin from here. As we have read, the beginning of this dynamic sees
the dual identity of the State as "Government" (a term that in the *Quaderni*
usually designates the institutional sphere in charge of political command)
and as "social society" (within the scope of private initiative). At first glance, it
is a situation that is difficult to understand (is not the institutional field *by definition* distinct from the social sphere?) and that Gramsci illustrates, though, in
the first part of the note where (just before the passage cited above) he refers

---

9   PN3: 75–76 (Q 6, § 88: 764).
10   Ibid.

to "the ultimate stages of 'economic-corporativism'" and an "economic-corporative form" characterized by "confusion between civil society and political society".[11]

One understands what Gramsci means by reading in synopsis a contemporary page from *Quaderno 8* ("Notebook 8") (the §185, precisely entitled "The economic-corporative phase of the state"[12]). Here, referring explicitly to the founding of a "new type of state", he clarifies what is inevitable ("no type of state can avoid going through [it]"): a first (and primitive) phase characterized, both by the inter-penetration between the institutional and social-economic spheres as well as by *the marked priority of economic politics*. The "political hegemony of the new social group that has founded the new type of state must be predominantly of an economic order".[13]

If we look carefully, this happens for an intuitive reason: a reason already underlying the Marxian texts previously mentioned. Dealing with the inaugural phase, the origin of the new "social formation", it is necessary first of all to consolidate the new structure: the new "relationships of production". The action of the "new social group" must therefore concentrate on the organization and consolidation of structural dynamics. Conversely, this makes it inevitable that cultural initiatives will be sacrificed. In this phase "the elements of the superstructure" (operating in the area of that "civil society" evoked in § 88 of *Quaderno 6*) "can only be weak"; "the cultural plan will be mostly negative: a critique of the past aimed at destruction and erasure of memory. Constructive policy will be still at the level of 'broad outlines', sketches".[14]

The essential information remains: the conquest of power by the new ruling class- in order to consolidate the successful outcome of the revolutionary shock – will follow a phase characterized as markedly authoritarian. Gramsci fully agrees with Lenin when he describes this phase as being inevitably long.

The theme of the long duration of the dictatorial phase is clearly described in another page of *Quaderno 6* ("Notebook 6"). In § 98, using his usual comparative mode, Gramsci observes that, *in general*, the type and breadth of duties entrusted to "the law" (compulsory rules) of the establishment of a new state power depends on the "different position occupied by the subaltern classes before becoming dominant".[15] Therefore, he points out that "certain subaltern classes, unlike others" (exactly because they *did not* previously occupy

---

11   PN3: 75 (Q 6, § 88: 763).
12   PN3: 342 (Q 8, §185: 1053).
13   Ibid.
14   Ibid.
15   PN3: 84 (Q 6, § 98: 773).

positions of power) should have a "long period of juridical intervention that is rigorous and then subdued".[16]

The allusion to the "position" of the working class in the bourgeois "old society" is transparent and allows us to draw the first conclusion. For the whole first long phase, the success of the workers' revolution (the consolidation of its initial results) involves, in Gramsci's view, the exercise of a strict coercive power, aimed essentially at defending the structural elements of the new social order. The dictatorship of the proletariat remains the key moment of revolutionary shock, the fundamental tool of the working class used for the construction of the "new society". We now arrive at the second question still remaining, which is closely connected to one just seen.

4   On the Extincion of the "Coercive State"

The initial situation is followed, in Gramsci's schema, by the phase of the "night-watchman state", in which the "element of coercive state" "gradually" reduces its own "authoritative and coercive interventions" (that is to say, "exhausts" itself) as soon as – *thanks to these interventions* (the process is dialectic) – on the contrary, energies and expressions of autonomy ("organic freedom") of "civil society" are developing: the "elements" of the new "regulated society".[17] What does this mean? What, in particular, corresponds to the concept of "night-watchman state" and "coercive state" and which relationships connect these two entities?

In the light of what we have considered so far regarding the functions of the workers' dictatorship, we can say that, while "coercive state" designates the state apparatus in that purely coercive organization (the "coercive state element" identifies the functions of the state responsible for the material exercise of "legal violence": the *military* moment of political domination); Lassalle's category of "night-watchman state" instead highlights the (gradual) *reduction* of "coercive measures" to protect the new economic dynamic, the new "mode of production".

Lassalle criticized the liberal theory of the "minimal" State, delegated only to the protection of bourgeois economic liberties. Now Gramsci takes up this idea again, certainly not to reevaluate the liberal schema (hence the warning to not "think of a new liberalism"[18]) but with the aim of highlighting, according

---

16   Ibid.
17   PN3: 75–76 (Q 6, § 88: 764).
18   Ibid.

to Lenin's model, the process of reducing the repressive component of the workers' new power in charge of supervising ("protecting") the results gradually achieved in the consolidation process ("continuous increase") of the new economic structure and the new system of social relationships.

As in Lenin,[19] for Gramsci, the task of the workers' State is twofold and ambivalent: it must on one hand protect the development of a "new society" and in this way is a *dictatorship*, the power of the people, "democracy" in its real sense, as Marx had provocatively written;[20] and, on the other hand, at the same time has to disappear, to become extinct as the "new society", under its armed protection, consolidates its own structures. Protect and extinguish; defend and "gradually reduce" their own "authoritarian and coercive interventions":[21] this is, both in the *Quaderni del carcere* ("Prison Notebooks") and in Государство и революция ("The State and Revolution"), the procedural function of the workers' state, the "dictatorship of the proletariat".

This is the theoretical architecture from which Gramsci reflects on the transition to Communism in the *Quaderni del carcere*. It is expressed in pages that form the ideal basis for focusing, in closing, the controversial question of Gramsci's judgment on the Soviet revolutionary experience, whose vicissitudes he follows until the end with unchanged passion.

5   The "de facto Power" of the "Political Party"

From many pages of the *Prison Notebooks* emerges the fact that Gramsci's theoretical research on the transition to communism intertwines with the reflection on what happens in these years in the Soviet Union. It is therefore worth asking what it represents, or more precisely, how it compares to the model of the transition to "regulated society" outlined in the *Quaderni del carcere* – the USSR between the end of the 1920s and the early 1930s, after the experience of the NEP (New Economic Policy) and the launch of the first five-year plan. To draft an answer to this question – which goes through most of the recent critical discussions – it is necessary to study four annotations found in *Quaderno 5* ("Notebook 5"), § 127, *Quaderno 7* ("Notebook 7"), § 43, *Quaderno 8* ("Notebook 8"), § 185 and *Quaderno 13* ("Notebook 13"),

---

19   Cf. Lenin 1974: 407 ff., 412–413, 482–484.
20   MEW 4: 481.
21   PN3: 75–76 (Q 6, § 88: 764).

§ 30. Here we limit ourselves to summing up some results of this synoptic reading.[22]

Even though Gramsci does not mention the Soviet Union in the first note (in homage to the caution that induces him to frequently resort to allusions, pseudonyms and paraphrases), it seems likely that this is the "new type of state" in question. If this hypothesis hits the mark, it is very interesting the way in which he values the "de facto power" which allows the "political party" (the Bolshevik Communist Party) to exercise the functions of the "head of state" ("the hegemonic function, and hence the function of balancing various interests"[23]). This is exactly the situation we have encountered working on § 88 of *Quaderno 6* (and on § 185 of *Quaderno 8*).

Gramsci writes that, "juridically" the "political party" in its operating as "head of the State", "neither rules nor governs".[24] But he immediately adds that, however, "in the reality of some States", it has "the de facto power" of reigning and governing, and this precisely by virtue of the close connection between "civil society" and "political society" that describes the first (and primitive) phase of the transition.

This situation, this close interpenetration of the political and social-economic planes – certainly contrary to "traditional constitutional law", but so made to allow the "political party" to "exercise the hegemonic function and thus balance different interests" – gives life (Gramsci writes) to a "reality which is in continuous movement"; where "it is not possible to create a constitutional law of the traditional type", but only "a system of principles asserting that the end of the state is its own end, its own disappearance: in other words, the reabsorption of political society into civil society".[25]

Therefore – assuming that we are in a new and dynamic political-juridical reality, ruled by a power that is not yet regulated – Gramsci records that the party exercises a "hegemonic function" (of political leadership, not of brute dominion), not only functional for the progressive extinction of the "state-coercion" but also recognized (and perhaps legitimized) by the "citizens" who "feel" that the party acts as "the head of state", as "the element that balances the various interests struggling against the predominant but not absolutely exclusivist interest".[26]

---

22   For an analytical treatment cf. Burgio 2018: 474–484.

23   PN2: 382 (Q 5, § 127: 662).

24   Ibid.

25   Ibid.

26   Ibid.

In the end, one could say that Gramsci sees in the Soviet Union at the early stages (necessarily characterized by the protagonism of coercive power) a reality "in continuous movement" which, *precisely by virtue of the use of instruments foreign to bourgeois constitutional law* (beyond which, it goes without saying, because of the inspiring finalities of the Bolshevik revolutionary experience), conforms to the model of the transition to a "new society" without classes and free from domination.

6 The Birth of a "New Civilization"

Any remaining doubt in this regard is lost when we consider two other texts that return to these same themes. Gramsci writes that the inaugural phase of the revolutionary process, inevitably concentrated on the economic dynamic, will only leave space for a meagre political culture, which will proceed by necessity with "'broad outlines', sketches that could (and should) be changed at all times in order to be consistent with the structure as it takes shape".[27] Curiously, he concludes:

> This, however, did not happen during the period of the communes. Instead, culture remained the function of the church; its character was, indeed, antieconomic (against the nascent capitalist economy); and its thrust was to prevent rather than enable the acquisition of hegemony by the new class. Humanism and the Renaissance were thus reactionary; they signaled the defeat of the new class, the negation of the economic world characterized by the new class, etc.[28]

What do the municipalities, humanism and the Renaissance have to do with the USSR? One understands reading this text in synopsis with the § 43 from *Quaderno 7* ("Notebook 7"), where Gramsci finally talks about the Soviet Union *apertis verbis* (and – even if he tries differently to support the contrary – in unambiguously commendatory terms).

Using one the many analogies that appear in the body of the *Quaderni del carcere*[29] ("Prison Notebooks"), Gramsci states that the "the process of the molecular formation of a new civilization currently under way may be compared

---

27   PN3: 342 (Q 8, §185: 1053).
28   Ibid.
29   On the importance of analogical reflection and comparative historical analysis in the theoretical context of the *Quaderni del carcere* cf. Burgio 2018: ch. 11.

to the Reformation movement".[30] Just as the Lutheran movement overturned the catholic concept of grace (fatalistic and a source of passivity) and infused a fervent spirit of initiative and promoted "on a worldwide scale" a "real practice of resourcefulness and initiative [...] that formed the ideology of a nascent capitalism" (here is the obvious echo of Weber); *in the same way*, where the "concept of historical materialism" (that "for many critics" should in principle generate "fatalism and passivity") becomes "reality", it inspires a passionate experience of social cooperation and collective resourcefulness: "it gives rise to a blossoming of initiatives and enterprises that astonish many observers"[31] (Gramsci gives the name of Michael Farbman, author of a supplement to the "Economist" on the first five-year plan).

There is no doubt that this note refers to the Soviet Union. The mention of Farbman's writing bears witness to the fact just as the explicit reference to "a study of the Union"[32] that should, in Gramsci's view, start from this type of comparative reflection. What he clearly argues here is that, in this way comparable to the "Reformation movement",[33] the Soviet experiment is actually succeeding in its intent to transform the life of an entire people thanks to an extraordinary "blossoming of initiatives and enterprises".[34] This is why it has to do with – and in 1930–32 it is not a negligible definition – a "process of the molecular formation of a new civilization".[35]

Nothing less. Whether it has to do with evaluations that were wrong in the early 1930s, now in hindsight, it is obvious. But anachronisms, instrumental uses and hurried conclusions – which could not only preclude the understanding of the texts, but also cause one to lose sight of the essential – must be avoided.

Rather, it is necessary, in our opinion, to hold two points firmly. First, the fact that, having been in prison for years, Gramsci knew very little about what was happening in the Soviet Union. In particular, he ignores the violence that accompanied the forced collectivization in the countryside, and knew nothing of the tragedy of the *kulak* between 1929 and 1932. This means that there is no sense in scrambling to prove the unprovable (that Gramsci looked at the Soviet Union with increasing aversion), for the simple reason that nothing leads to the revocation of the conviction that a "new civilization" was emerging in the "Union".

30   PN3: 193 (Q 7, §44: 892).
31   Ibid.
32   Ibid.
33   Ibid.
34   Ibid.
35   Ibid.

Secondly, on methodological grounds, one must keep clearly in mind the distance that in every context separates historical or political judgment from theoretical discourse. What Gramsci writes, reasoning on the theory of historical transitions and in particular on the transition to Communism, does not depend on his reflection on the Soviet experience even though undoubtedly these reflections and the judgement that he formed on the "new type" of State born of the Bolshevik revolution contribute to giving shape to the theoretical elaboration. Indeed, what remains most important is the collection of concepts and paradigms used to construct this theoretical elaboration: elements that Gramsci took with full awareness from Marx and Lenin, not without reworking them into an original theory, in harmony with the times.

Bibliography

Gramsci's Works and Abbreviations
Gramsci, A. (1982), *La città futura. 1917–1918*, Caprioglio, S. (ed.) (Torino: Einaudi).
Gramsci, A. (1987), *L'Ordine Nuovo. 1919–1920*, Gerratana, V., Santucci, A.A. (eds.) (Torino: Einaudi).
PN: Buttigieg, J.A. (ed.) (1992, 1996, 2007), *Prison Notebooks* (New York: Columbia University Press), 3 vols.
Q: Gerratana, V. (ed.) (1975), *Quaderni del carcere* (Torino: Einaudi), 4 vols.
SPN: Hoare, Q., Nowell-Smith, G. (eds.) (1971), *Selection from the Prison Notebooks* (New York: International Publishers).
SPW-1: Hoare, Q., Nowell Smith, G. (eds.) (1977), *Selections from Political Writings, 1910–1920* (London: Lawrence & Wishart; New York: International Publisher).

Other Works
Burgio, A. (2003), *Gramsci storico. Una lettura dei "Quaderni del carcere"* (Roma-Bari: Laterza).
Burgio, A. (2014), *Gramsci. Il sistema in movimento* (Roma: DeriveApprodi).
Burgio, A. (2018), *Il sogno di una cosa. Per Marx* (Roma: DeriveApprodi).
Lenin, V.I. (1974), *Staat und Revolution*, in Lenin, V.I., *Werke*, vol. 25 (Berlin: Dietz).
MEW: Marx, K., Engels, F., *Marx-Engels Werke*, 44 vol. (Berlin: Dietz).

PART 4

Hegemony

∵

CHAPTER 9

Gramsci: Political Scientist

Michele Prospero

Of central importance in Gramsci is the theoretical-interpretive grid based on the moment of difference (State-society) and the moment of mediation (representation, subjects, organizations). Modern politics, in which an abstract and separate sphere from the State transcends the corporatism of micro-interests and bypasses the localism of small territories, cannot rest on the atomism of individuals who roam autonomously and without ties or processes of mobilization. Recognizing a debt with Hegel, Gramsci substitutes the dyadic relationship of abstract state/unrelated individual, with a more flexible scheme that uses mediation as a connecting bridge between the general-representative sphere and the economic-particular sphere. This is the moment of representation that, from the social and its fractures, organizes subjectivities by equipping them with collective expressions and projects them onto the field of political confrontation. Civil society does not coincide with the economy in a separate space, and it is not the photography of individuals such as atoms without interdependencies.

The unity of the state and civil society signifies that both manifestations of this explicative couple are methodologically differentiated parts of a broader system. This unity may have progressive forms, and eversion of ownership relations but also the face of conservation with the conferment to the State of the minimum tasks of acting as custodian of the proprietary order. In a system such as the modern one – which sees the unity of the State and of society – both moments of public intervention in the economy as well as moments of deregulation and liberalism are possible. These contingent politics do not evoke the reabsorption of the separation of State and society that continue to operate as the backbone of modernity. For Gramsci, within the framework of the unity of the modern social system (which integrates abstract politics and market economy), it is possible for analytical purposes to understand the conceptual separation of State and society.

This combination of the unity of the social mechanism, expressed in the differentiation of its functions, escapes from the principal theoretical currents. The distinction between State and society then loses analytical rigor and becomes a mask of ideology. For the liberals, civil society means economic activity – private forces and the State propose itself as the rule of law. The figure of the minimal State that monopolizes public goods is thus presented and this minimal state entrusts the care of the particular interest to the market. The moment of the public appears, warns Gramsci, as

> a State whose functions are limited to the safeguarding of public order and respect for the laws. The fact is glossed over that in this form of régime (which anyways has never existed except on paper, as a limiting hypothesis) hegemony over its historical developments belongs to private forces, to civil society – which is "State" too, indeed is the State itself.[1]

The dilation of the distance between private and public, in the name of the autonomy of the economic calculation, is also the result of a political decision that designates a particular extension of the relationship between State and society. Politics is the decision that shortens the gap between State and society just like politics is also the decision that enlarges the distance between public and private. Not only liberals, but also Catholics embody an ideological vision of the relationship between State and society. "They would like to have the interventionist state on their side; failing that, they want a neutral state because an unfavorable state might support their enemies. In reality, the Catholics want everything to be in their favor".[2] The State is indifferent or minimal to others while it is clearly recognizable as a visible hand when it protects certain interests and values.

Skeptical of the central-bureaucratic State, what is relevant in catholic thought is the horizontal profile, the relationship supportive neighborhood, and "the town council was traditionally considered civil society and not state".[3] Civil society becomes the place of exchange and a reticular leading role of associated worlds: the horizontal link of particularism that creates connections in an interpenetration between economic-proprietary instances and the cult of the periphery as a place of communitarian authenticity. A certain combination of Catholic culture and the exaltation of particularism, Gramsci notes,

> it directs its attention toward the "particular", toward the bourgeois as an individual who develops within civil society and who has no conception of political society outside his "particular" sphere. It is tied to Guelfism,

---

1   SPN: 261 (Q 26, § 6: 2302). Cf. Poulantzas 1975; Buci-Glucksmann 1976; Carnoy 1984.
2   PN2: 328 (Q 5, § 69: 604). Cf. Bellamy, Schecter 1993.
3   PN1: 215 (Q 1, § 130: 118). Cf. Morera 1990.

which can be said to be a medieval theoretical syndicalism. It is federalist without having a federal center.[4]

A manifestation of unresolved dualism is found in Catholic culture that sets the periphery against the center, the world of community living against the vertical rigidity of power.

Gramsci notices an affinity between the catholic views that magnify the foreignness of the peripheries from the center, and the socialist tendencies to operate within the spaces of society's real life against structure of the liberal regime. The Italian example is presented as a contraposition (high-low, power-society) that proceeds due to the lack of subjects of mediation between the élite and the people. For Gramsci, mediation is the construction of an efficient connection between society and state that is indispensable for the governance of modernization. The analysis of social conflicts and territorial fractures in the history of the liberal state lead Gramsci to point out the limits of a political élite that is incapable of conferring a social base to long term strategies and thus is incapable of governing the recomposition of these spaces (which include interests, beliefs and faith). For Gramsci, the nationalization of the masses and territorial amalgamation pass through the politics of the élite capable of connecting interests, culture, and political-institutional planning. The weight of the original fractures, on the other hand, imprint a sign of weakness, based on support and capacity for integration, on the liberal regime that is upset by the politicization of class conflict (communist unionism) and by the organization of Catholics first in civil society (white syndicalism) and then in the political (confessional party). The Gramscian scrutiny highlights the failure of the elite to set up mediation between state and society, confirmed as an insurmountable condition for starting the processes of modernity.

Without the organized pluralism of a dense civil society, anti-political suggestions proliferate which disorient a system that does not know how to project itself beyond the findings of powerless transformism anchored to a static parliamentary framework. For Gramsci, when the subjects of mediation fail, a charismatic solution can prevail with the myth of the lightning decision that suspends the rites of representation in the name of the achieved social homogeneity. As a mixture of interests and rules "political society and civil society are a single entity"[5] but this should not be understood in the sense of Gentile for which the state or government-force is the whole. It is not possible to

---

4   PN2: 338 (Q 5, § 85: 614). Cf. De Rosa 1978; Bellamy 1994.
5   PN2: 182 (Q 4, § 38: 460). Cf. Bobbio 1978, 1990; Texier 1968; Haugaard, Lentner 2006; Martin 2015.

confirm the regained unity (substantial, ethical-political) of society and state because the material assets continue to operate according to the logic of accumulation and the forms of power register exclusions of pluralism and coercive measures that reveal the absence of any real recomposition. After having formulated the request of enlargement beyond the dimension of the force to grasp the link between the heterogeneous, Gramsci raises the contextual demand for differentiation, for which we must distinguish within the concept of State between "civil society and political society, between hegemony and dictatorship".[6]

The ambition to overcome parliamentarianism (caught in structural difficulty before the tasks of social integration) with corporate grafts is destined for failure in Gramsci's view. Rather than on the institutional side, in which functional representation cannot be considered as a solid alternative to individualistic representation, corporatism is interesting for its profile of economic policy oriented to forms of innovation from above with the ambition of stopping conflict and absorbing the hardships for the purposes of conservation. Gramsci analyses the ideological intentions of corporatism to define with public leverage the indispensable material for a productive industrial bloc – to allocate the use of savings in the direction of market growth and rising salaries. The corporate challenge to Americanism (innovation, reduction of costs, efficient management of complexity within companies, involvement of the union in practices of subaltern approval) does not take off in Italy with efficiency and coherence because fascism, in its effort to operate that strong institutional axis to favor capitalistic modernization, rejects the face of the liberal state, free competition, the autonomy of social subject and the instances of conflict.

The preservation of the structures of economic-social power is the trait of the fascist experience, which thinks of interventions to use the savings for investment purposes but fails to give organic capacity to govern the novelty and to relaunch the productive forces and with them the internal demand. More than a public factor that plans development, Fascism appears as a controlling body that fights unemployment by taking measures to contain social problems with procedures that are only useful in the short term. For Gramsci, it is precisely in this role of authoritative control of discomfort that fascism takes the form of a static regime aimed at the middle classes and at the maintenance of threatened interests. The role of the state is thus reabsorbed into police functions and not aimed at development, innovation, technical-business organization, rationalization of costs and processes. Gramsci excluded the possibility

---

6 SPN: 271 (Q 6, § 10: 691). Cf. Tamburrano 1963; Bonetti 1980; Belligni 1981; Martelli 1996; Bellamy 2013; Rosengarten 2014.

that the corporate regime might in fact turn out to be a factor of real innovation in the long term. While Americanism implicates the figures of the liberal
state, fascism assumes a closed social and institutional attitude, restrictive to
the point of harnessing competition in order to preserve an authoritarian social discipline, breaking some basic regularities that seem to pervade the modern experience.

In the regimes of the masses, the overcoming of the conceptual distinction
between state and society through the one-party government or "bureaucratic
solution" is apparent. For this, the moment of mediation and representation
remains open and not susceptible to mythical solutions. Both change and conservation raise the question of political mediation. There exists politics of
management/administration ("this question has to do with the rotation in governmental power of different fractions from the same dominant group") and
politics of change ("the foundation and organization of a new political society,
much less of a new type of civil society"[7]). Both of these manifestations of politics lead back to the story of representation and to the institutes of mediation
which seem destined to persist, with adaptations and grafts, until the distinction between public and private, society and state remains. In the context of a
certain defining oscillation in the use of the principal terms, Gramsci outlines
an open interpretative scheme with three relevant dimensions. The state,
which is not only the state-government that administers the governing force,
but also presents itself as a broad state or community – as a unity with the
characteristics of civil society.

In this sense, the state is not only government or a sanctioning apparatus
that "is commonly understood as the entire state"[8] but is also life and society.
In civil society, Gramsci does not only see the signs of economic relationships
but also the typical dynamics of political-cultural character. In the time of the
mobilization of civil society with plural subjects, the State loses its "being for
itself", which projects it as an abstract dimension of power. It presents an enlarged political dimension that goes beyond the state. It is a broad layer of civil
society, which goes beyond the economic, to host an organized pluralism. Political society as state is the law, regulation and the coercive expression of domination. Civil society, on the other hand, is the way of existing and producing
the objective conditions of living where economic struggles and the conquest
of hegemony are found with the discoveries of politics and culture. Given this
intersection of public and social, Gramsci arrives at the hypothesis that in
statehood, we see actors different than the administration and forms (the

---

7   PN2: 183 (Q 4, § 38: 460–461).
8   PN3: 310 (Q 8, § 130: 1020).

parties) and in civil society we do not only trace the footsteps of the economy but also the symbols of subjectivity (parties and unions). In some ways, the parties introduce social profiles into the political system and impose public determinations in the private sphere.

Gramsci alludes to a sphere that is larger than the State-administrator of violence and postulates an opening to the complex superstructure of civil society.

> What we can do, for the moment, is to fix two major superstructural "levels": the one that can be called "civil society", that is the ensemble of organisms commonly called "private", and that of "political society" or "the State". These two levels correspond on the one hand to the function of "hegemony" which the dominant group exercises throughout society and on the other hand to that of "direct domination" or command exercised through the State and "juridical" government.[9]

Considering the composition of civil society, which hosts material structures but also collective organizations with general political projection, it is indispensable for Gramsci to extend the idea of super-structural plans. On one hand, civil society is made up of family, neighborhood and "social relationships". On the other hand, moments of collective pressure, customs, relational forms not determined by sanction, ways of thinking and superstitions can emerge in civil society. The ability to resist the system in the face of economic and social crisis also depends on the construction of connecting networks and beliefs which preserve the social order even without direct coercive intervention.

Not on the basis of the complete conceptual definition of terms, but on that of reflection of historical-political issues, emerges a broad idea of state that opens towards society (State-community) and expands into the world of organized subjects (political society). From Gramsci's perspective, the conceptual framework appears as "mediated by two types of social organization: (*a*) by civil society, that is, by the ensemble of private organizations in society; (*b*) by the State".[10] Civil society, more than a dimension made up of individuals, is a structure of many organizations that relate to each other and the moment of statehood. Civil society is also the individual, but taken is his role of *socius* who associates in worldly experiences and organizes himself into a group. Without a dense network of subjects of mediation placed between society and state, the regimes of the masses do not consolidate and in consequence the institutions

---

9   SPN: 12 (Q 12, § 1: 1518–1519). Cf. Finocchiaro 1988.
10   PN2: 200 (Q 4, § 49: 476). Cf. Femia 2002; Haugaard, Lentner 2006; Coutinho 2012.

of government show themselves to be ephemeral entities without support and exposed to destructive myths or charismatic seductions. Fascism was also a problem born of land and class. While France managed the crisis with state resources (the long duration of central power) with a richer panorama of parties, with a more solid civic culture (the mobilizing power of the Marseillaise), Italy struggled with the weakness of its state-party-civic system. In the countryside of Italy is seen the reemergence of master-servant polarity that provoked panic in landowning areas threatened by revolt, strikes and occupations. In France, widespread small farm landowners had instead averted the radicalization of the conflict thus depriving the populist right of a valuable base of support among the agrarians.

For Gramsci, the term populism means the tendency to call on the people assumed in its indeterminacy, or postulating mythical unity and absence of conflicts within a fictitious community. This is found in the "exaltation of the popular masses in general, with all their basic needs (food, clothing, shelter, reproduction)".[11] An appeal to the people, and to certain "elementary critical feelings" that the people invent as a homogeneous entity, is certainly an ideological tool to stop the proletariat as a factor that differentiates or imposes partitions. According to Gramsci, in populism (recognizable in Mazzini and Pisacane, in French literature and in the myth of the simple) there is also a hidden form of democracy – an instance of reaching a more substantial and less formal organization of power as compared with liberal-constitutional one because it is open to real sensibilities. Populism refers to the concept of the people as a homogenous entity, matured before the organization of class. It contains democracy as it was configured before 1848, when the people as a presupposed unity passed to the difference of people segmented into classes. For Gramsci, a people that is compact and unified is not a realistic fact. "Public opinion is the political content of the public's political will that can be dissentient".[12] Conflict exists, not homogeneity. With these new dynamics of conflict, economic data and the subjectivity of politics are fused, rendering the unitarian concept of the people anachronistic. The political party of the masses as organization that "efficiently" fuses groups and intellectual classes introduces difference, and breaks the binomial state as the sole interpreter of politics and the people, described as a generic entity.[13]

A reality such as the political party, that is both civil society and political society, introduces moments of connection between the subjects, which break

---

11   PN3: 118 (Q 6, § 157: 812).

12   PN3: 213 (Q 7, § 83: 915). Cf. Haugaard, Lentner 2006.

13   Cf. Paggi 1970.

the symbolism of populism. When the connection-differentiation between society and state breaks down, problems of subversion emerge. Even if not always in conceptually controlled forms ("if the state – even in its wider sense of civil society"[14]), the scheme of the methodical distinction between State and society, and with it the need for mediation, is crucial in Gramsci. In his recognition the State-society distinction as a rigid dual axis is overpassed by the huge transformation that provides a hinging function, a function of intermediation between parties ("the parties were precisely the organisms that not only developed political guidelines in civil society but also educated and presented men supposed to be able to apply them"[15]). With the parties, it is also the structure of representative institutions that assigns tasks of political-state direction of general constitutional importance to organized subjects of society. In the parliamentary regime, the interest becomes state-centered,

> because the parliamentary group of the strongest party became the "government" or led the government. The fact that, due to parliamentary disintegration, the parties have become incapable of carrying out this task did not cancel the task itself nor did it show a new way towards a solution: the same thing applies to education and the enhancement of personalities.[16]

The crisis of the parliamentary system and of traditional political parties destroys the balancing mechanism of mediation. In the face of the erosion of political forms, the nostalgic action of mourning the institutional balances broken by irreversible processes is in vain.

With respect to other organized groups who operate in society and mobilize themselves in the face of conflict, political parties organize themselves like organisms that, although established in the social sphere, carry out general tasks and contribute in the management of the resources of power and coercion. The ambiguous nature of the political party emerges in this way. As private organizations, political parties are societies, as government apparatuses, they are instead like the state or a political society. The party, although it exists in society, develops public tasks and for this reason it appears to Gramsci as "the mechanism that carries out in civil society the same function that the state

---

14   FSPN: 64 (Q 16, § 11: 1869).
15   Q 15, § 48: 1809; untranslated in English. Cf. Mastellone, Sola 2001; von Beyme 2013; Martin 2015.
16   Ibid.

carries out, to a greater extent, in political society".[17] Thus, in its attributions, the State is not different from the political society of which it is the principal expression and the political party is a profile of civil society which tends, however, to extend itself in the plan of the state and as a depositary body of political tasks of a more restricted degree shown to expand functions and tools. The tendency is to reshape the directive centrality of the state as a coercive body of political society and therefore to define a wider political society than the State following the multiplication of social actors who perform political tasks.

The political party occupies formerly state functions and determines connections between the social and the political.

> In reality, in certain sense, the "head of state" – that is, the element that balances the various interests struggling against the predominant but not absolutely exclusivistic interest – is precisely the "political party". With the difference, however, that in terms of traditional constitutional law the political party juridically neither rules nor governs. It has "de facto power", it exercises the hegemonic function, and hence the function of balancing various interests, in "civil society"; however, "civil society" is in fact so thoroughly intertwined with political society that all the citizens fell instead that the party rules and governs.[18]

After the consolidation of the parties, the changes in the liberal state are not, according to Gramsci, comprehensible with the traditional models of constitutional law anchored in the public-private, legal-factual dualism. The three-dimensional explanatory diagram sees the interaction between the state (juridical form, the moment of sovereignty and of organized coercion in a monopolistic way) civil society (distinct within an area of economy, and in the levels of action or molecular processes of associative life) and enlarged political society (the moment of contention, the competition between many actors that open channels of intersection between the social and the institutional). Unions and political parties (that postulate "a strong center of political leadership") are the components of civil society where Gramsci places that distinctive trait of modernity which separates the functional ambit and abstract from the particular, while at the same time, demands the presence of the subjects of pluralism – of actors in a conflict for hegemony that embraces values and interests, economy and cultural politics.

---

17   PN2: 202 (Q 4, § 49: 477–478); Liguori 2019.
18   PN2: 382 (Q 5, § 127: 662).

With Americanism, capitalism throws down a challenge, transcending the limits of its own economic doctrine that (from the classics to marginalize) exclude the collective movement of workers as a disturbing factor and brings back the high salaries to inflation and inevitable unemployment because of dwindling profit and investment margins. The union (the collective subject), absent from classic economic theory, becomes crucial for Gramsci in determining policies for growth. Unions (social action) and the political party (projects) should unite. The supremacy of the party in the complex definition of a collective consciousness, conforming with the political tradition of Europe in the 1900s, is accompanied by the recognition of the function of the union: in the instances of social representation and in the rhythms of a struggle that does not stop at the economic dimension. Class (fundamental social conflict) and people (majority consensus) must be integrated. Gramsci sees the role of political culture as a way to connect an analysis of class (diagnosis of modern capitalism) and the political construction of a people with the resources of hegemony (alliances, antagonistic social bloc). Primacy of the political (or hegemonic dimension) and autonomy of the social (conflict, even spontaneous mobilization) seem to mark Gramsci's reasoning, which goes in search of a subjectivity articulated and endowed with a critical conscience. In this context, the political party is central in proposing itself as a vehicle for culture, organization and languages.

> In reality, every political movement creates a language of its own, that is, it participates in the general development of a distinct language, introducing new terms, enriching existing terms with a new content, creating metaphors, using historical names to facilitate the comprehension and the assessment of particular contemporary political situations.[19]

A political party of the masses does not rest solely on the economic element. A project in harmony with an epochal change is needed, in the relationship between the territory of politics (national) and the economic space (global). Gramsci cautions the "greater autonomy of the national economies from the economic relations of the world market".[20] This weakening of political sovereignty makes it difficult to stage a revolution in a single country, forced to live with a world economy dominated by trade and by the regime of capital. But also the fate of the war of position is consigned to a strategic asymmetry between the profile of sovereignty (limited in the national dimension) and the degree of interdependence imposed by the elusive dynamics of the world market.

19   PN1: 126 (Q 2, § 43: 31). Cf. Ives 2004; Boothman 2011; Carlucci 2013.
20   SPN: 243 (Q 13, § 7: 1566). Cf. Cox 1993; Ayers 2008.

Bibliography

Gramsci's Works and Abbreviations

FSPN: Boothman, D. (ed.) (1995), *Further Selections from the Prison Notebooks* (Minneapolis: Minnesota University Press).

PN: Buttigieg, J.A. (ed.) (1992, 1996, 2007), *Prison Notebooks* (New York: Columbia University Press), 3 vols.

Q: Gerratana, V. (ed.) (1975), *Quaderni del carcere* (Torino: Einaudi), 4 vols.

SPN: Hoare, Q., Nowell-Smith, G. (eds.) (1971), *Selection from the Prison Notebooks* (New York: International Publishers).

Other Works

Ayers, A.J. (ed.) (2008), *Gramsci, Political Economy, and International Relations Theory* (New York: Palgrave Macmillan).

Bellamy, R. (1994), *Introduction*, in A. Gramsci, *Pre-Prison Writings* (New York: Cambridge University Press).

Bellamy, R. (2013), *Croce, Gramsci, Bobbio and the Italian Political Tradition* (Lanham: Rowman & Littlefield).

Bellamy, R., Schecter, D. (1993), *Gramsci and the Italian State* (Manchester: Manchester University Press).

Belligni, S. (1981), *Egemonia*, in N. Bobbio, N. Matteucci (ed.) *Dizionario di politica* (Torino: Utet).

Bobbio, N. (1978), *Stato, governo, società* (Torino: Einaudi).

Bobbio, N. (1990), *Saggi su Gramsci* (Milano: Feltrinelli).

Bonetti, P. (1980), *Gramsci e la società liberaldemocratica* (Roma-Bari: Laterza).

Boothman, D. (2013), *The Sources for Gramsci's Concept of Hegemony*, in Green, M.E. (ed.), *Rethinking Gramsci* (London: Routledge).

Buci-Glucksmann, C. (1976), *Gramsci e lo Stato* (Roma: Editori Riuniti).

Carlucci, A. (2013), *Gramsci and Languages* (Boston-Leiden: Brill).

Carnoy, M. (1984), *The State and Political Theory* (Princeton: Princeton University Press).

Coutinho, C.N. (2012), *Gramsci's Political Thought* (Boston-Leiden: Brill).

Cox, R.W. (1993), *Gramsci, Hegemony and International Relations*, in Gill, S. (ed.), *Gramsci, Historical Materialism and International Relations* (Cambridge: Cambridge University Press).

De Rosa, G. (1978), *Gramsci e la questione cattolica*, in Ferri, F. (ed.), *Politica e storia in Gramsci* (Roma: Editori Riuniti).

Femia, J.V. (2002), *Hegemony and Consciousness in the Thought of Antonio Gramsci*, in Martin, J. (ed.), *Gramsci. Critical Assessments of Leading Political Philosophers* (London: Routledge).

Finocchiaro, M.A. (1988), *Gramsci and the History of Dialectical Thought* (Cambridge: Cambridge University Press).

Haugaard, M., Lentner, H.H. (2006), *Hegemony and Power* (Oxford: Lexington Books).

Ives, P. (2004), *Gramsci's Politics of Language* (Toronto: University of Toronto Press).

Liguori, G. (2019), *Gramsci e il populismo* (Milano: Unicopli).

Martelli, M. (1996), *Gramsci filosofo della politica* (Milano: Unicopli).

Martin, J. (2015), *Morbid Symptoms: Gramsci and the Crisis of Liberalism*, in McNally, M., *Antonio Gramsci* (London: Palgrave MacMillan).

Mastellone, S., Sola, G. (eds.) (2001), *Gramsci: il partito politico nei "Quaderni"* (Firenze: CET).

Morera, E. (1990), *Gramsci's Historicism. A Realist Interpretation* (London: Routledge).

Paggi, L. (1970), *Gramsci e il moderno principe* (Roma: Editori Riuniti).

Poulantzas, N. (1975), *Potere politico e classi sociali* (Roma: Editori Riuniti).

Rosengarten, F. (2014), *The Revolutionary Marxism of Antonio Gramsci* (Boston-Leiden: Brill).

Tamburrano, G. (1963), *Antonio Gramsci* (Manduria: Lacaita Editore).

Texier, J. (1968), *Gramsci teorico delle sovrastrutture e il concetto di società civile*, in "Critica marxista", 3, pp. 71–99.

von Beyme, K. (2013), *Sozialismus* (Berlin: Springer).

CHAPTER 10

The "Prison Notebooks": Hegemony and Civil Society

Giuseppe Cospito

Before addressing the main theme of my presentation, a methodological introduction is necessary: the following pages are placed in the furrow of the recent additions to Gramscian historiography and philology. They have two points of departure: on one side, the substantial continuity – both within a constantly evolving framework and also in relation to the dramatic national and international historical developments – of Gramsci's reflection before and during his incarceration; and on the other side the possibility and the necessity to follow this evolution even within a short period of time (1929–1935): the time of his reflections in prison.[1]

As highlighted in the most recent literature,[2] Gramsci's reflection on hegemony resumes in prison after having being forcibly interrupted at the end of 1926 when he (then Secretary of the Communist Party of Italy) was arrested even while being formally protected by parliamentary immunity as a member of Parliament. A few weeks earlier, Gramsci had written a letter – destined to become famous – to the Central Committee of the Bolshevik Communist Party where he maintained, in conflict with the narrow concept of political power that united both the Stalinist majority and the Trotskyist minority, that "the proletariat cannot become the dominant class" except through the "sacrifice of corporate interests [...], it cannot maintain its hegemony and its dictatorship if, even becoming dominant, it does not sacrifice these immediate interests for the general and permanent interests of the class".[3] This acceptance of hegemony reestablished the Leninist formula that Gramsci had adopted beginning in March 1924, when he commemorated the recently deceased leader, affirming:

> Bolshevism is the first, in the international history of class struggle, to have developed the idea of hegemony of the proletariat and to have

1 Cf. Cospito 2016 and the critical literature discussed within.
2 Cf. Vacca 2017: Chapter I.
3 Gramsci 1971: 129–130.

practically placed the principal revolutionary problems that Marx and
Engels had presented theoretically. The idea of the hegemony of the proletariat, exactly because it is understood historically and concretely, has
brought with it the necessity for the working class to find an ally. Bolshe-
vism found this ally in the masses of poor peasants. [...] The peasant cannot conquer the land without the help of the worker; the worker cannot
overthrow capitalism without the help of the peasant. Politically, the
worker is stronger and more capable than the peasant. He lives in the city,
is concentrated in large numbers in the factories, and is able to not only
overthrow capitalism but also to impede (by socializing industry) the return of capitalism. This is why revolution presents itself practically as a
hegemony of the proletariat that guides its ally – the peasants.[4]

Going back even further, if not the term *hegemony*, that in the writings preceding his stay in Moscow (May 1922-November 1923) appears exclusively as in the
then currently accepted meaning of supremacy, the concept is at least implicitly present from the period of the "Ordine Nuovo" ("New Order"). Gramsci recalls the concept in the essay on the *Quistione meridionale* ("Southern question") left unpublished at the time of his arrest, writing that:

The Turin communists had concretely posed the question of the "hegemony of the proletariat", that is, the question of the social base of the
proletarian dictatorship and the workers' state. The proletariat can become the ruling class and dominant in the way in which it manages to
create a system of class alliances that allows it to mobilize the majority of
the working population against capitalism and the bourgeois state, which
means, in the existing class relations in Italy, to the extent that it is able to
obtain the consent of the large peasant masses.[5]

Gramsci would resume his theoretical writings more than two years later, at
the end of a long judicial procedure (arrest, confinement, preventive incarceration, prosecution and conviction of more than 20 years in prison, request
to obtain the permission to write while imprisoned). The *Quaderno 1* ("Notebook 1") bears the date of February 8th, 1929, but for a whole year the prisoner
merely formulates some work plans and drafts a handful of annotations of bibliographical nature, dedicating the rest of his time to reading and above all,

---

4   Gramsci: 1924, pp. 2 4.
5   Gramsci 1971: 139–140.

translating hundreds of pages from German and Russian.[6] It is only between February and March of 1930 that what can be defined as an "explosion" occurs in Gramsci's theoretical-political reflections, placing hegemony again at the center of his thoughts where he had left it at the end of 1926. In § 44 of *Notebook 1*, significantly entitled *Direzione politica di classe prima e dopo l'andata al governo* ("Political Class leadership before and after assuming government power"), we read that:

> The politico-historical criterion on which our own inquiries must be grounded is this: that a class is dominant in two ways, namely it is "leading" and "dominant". It leads the allied classes, it dominates the opposing classes. Therefore, a class can (and must) "lead" even before assuming power; when it is in power it becomes dominant, but it also continues to "lead". [...] There can and there must be a "political hegemony" even before assuming government power, and in order to exercise political leadership or hegemony one must not count solely on the power and material force that is given by government.[7]

This formulation, and others similar to it, on one hand, sometimes take on almost literal expressions used by Gramsci in the last phase of his active political militancy and in particular in the essay on the *Quistione meridionale* ("Southern question"), while on the other hand introduces a series of innovations destined to connote the prison reflections in a different way. First of all, consistent with the forcefully *für ewig* character of Gramsi's writing in those years, what was a political strategy in a certain phase, later becomes a *political-historical* criterion; consequently, it is not only the question of the hegemony of the proletariat that is at stake here, but of any social class – in the second draft of the *Notebook 19*, § 24, Gramsci will say social *group* – that tries to conquer and conserve power. Furthermore, already at this point there is an apparent oscillation between a narrow sense of hegemony intended as rule based on consensus and a broader definition: hegemony understood as rule *and* domination – consent that is not opposed to force. That which seems to be one of the

---

6 Cf. *Genesi e svolgimento del lavoro in carcere* in Cospito, Frosini 2017: XX et seq.

7 PN1: 136–137 (Q 1, § 44: 41). Since the new critical edition of Gramsci's *Quaderni* (*Prison Notebooks*) referred to in the previous note, is still in the finishing stages, from now on the reference to the prison manuscripts will be in the order of the notebooks and paragraphs proposed in V. Gerratana (ed.) (1975), *Quaderni del carcere* (Turin: Einaudi) even where this does not correspond to that of the new edition. For the dates of single prison notes cf. Cospito 2011: 896–904.

numerous Gramscian antimonies,[8] can only be explained if we keep in mind the distinction, proposed by Gramsci in § 48 of *Notebook 1*, between "the 'normal' exercise of hegemony on the now classic terrain of the parliamentary regime", which appears to be "characterized by a combination of force and consent which balance each other so that force does not overwhelm consent but rather appears to be backed by the consent of the majority, expressed by the so-called organs of public opinion", and situations in which "the hegemonic apparatus cracks and the exercise of hegemony becomes ever more difficult. The phenomenon is presented and discussed in various terms and from different points of view. The most common are 'crisis of the principle of authority', 'dissolution of the parliamentary regime'".[9] Gramsci writes an analogous discourse in § 61 for those political structures (like in the United States) that find themselves still in "the phase of psycho-physical adaptation to the new industrial structure", where "there has not yet been (except sporadically, perhaps) any 'superstructural' blossoming; therefore, the fundamental question of hegemony has not yet been posed".[10] In § 185 of *Quaderno 8* ("Notebook 8", December 1931), these considerations are extended to each state entity, past present and future (with clear reference also to the nascent Soviet socialist state) where Gramsci speaks of the "*economic-corporative phase of the state*. If it is true that no type of state can avoid passing through a phase of economic-corporative primitivism, one can deduce that the content of the political hegemony of the new social group that has founded the new type of state must be predominantly of an economic order. This would entail the reorganization of the structure and of the real relations between people and the sphere of the economy or of production".[11]

Gramsci's reflection on the concept of *civil society* begins between February and March 1930. Unlike hegemony, this term does not belong to the lexicon of Gramsci's writings preceding his imprisonment. In fact, it only appears two times: in an article from 1918, paraphrasing a text by the physiocrat Le Trosne[12] and in an article from the "Ordine Nuovo" of May 1921, in which the goal of the nascent fascist movement is identified in the destruction of the minimal civil society present in Italy, in order to promote the aims of the national and

---

8 The reference is obviously to Anderson 2017 which confirms the thesis of the first edition of the essay (1976), despite the theoretical and philological refutation in the second part of Francioni 1984.

9 PN1: 155–156 (Q 1, § 48: 59).

10 PN1: 169 (Q 1, § 61: 72).

11 PN3: 342 (Q 8, § 185: 1053).

12 NM: 172.

international capital.[13] In this second occurrence, the connection between hegemony and civil society appears in a nutshell that would only be developed during the course of his reflections in prison. The term appears here for the first time in § 130 of *Quaderno 1* ("Notebook 1", February-March 1930), in relation to the way in which Italian Catholics used the term in the first decades of the unified national state, from the breach of Porta Pia to *non expedit:*

> *Real Italy and legal Italy.* The formula contrived by the clericals after 1870 to direct attention to the national political uneasiness: contradiction between legal Italy and real Italy. [...] Generally speaking, it is felicitous because there existed a clear disjunction between the *state* (legality) and *civil society* (reality) – but did this *civil society* exist completely and exclusively within "clericalism"? Meanwhile, this same *civil society* was something shapeless and chaotic and remained so for many decades; it was therefore possible for the *state* to dominate it, overcoming each time the contradictions that presented themselves in a sporadic, localized form, without any national nexus.[14]

The development of Gramsci's prison reflections would result in negating the real character of this contradiction, deepening the meaning of the expression *civil society.* This is, however, affirmed with difficulty in Gramsci's own vocabulary, as seen in the translations he made of Marx's texts (in *Notebook 7*, beginning in May 1930 and continuing through 1931) where the 22 occurrences of *bürgerliche Gesellschaft* are translated as *società borghese* (bourgeois society) and in only two cases later corrected to read *società civile* (civil society); both recurring in a passage of the preface of 1859 to *Zur Kritik der politischen Ökonomie* ("A Contribution to the Critique of Political Economy"), that Gramsci translates: "both juridical relationships as well as state forms [...] are rooted in the material relationships of life, that Hegel, following the English and French of the 18th century, embraced with the name 'civil society'; but [...] the anatomy of civil society is to be found in political economy".[15] This last idea would be revisited by Gramsci in the first note especially dedicated to the subject in § 24 of *Notebook 6*:

> *Encyclopedic notions. Civil society.* One must distinguish civil society as Hegel understands it and in the sense it is *often* [our italics] used in these

---

13   SPW-1: 44–45 (Gramsci 1967: 167–169).

14   PN1: 214 (Q 1, § 130: 117).

15   Gramsci 2007: 745.

notes (that is, in the sense of the political and cultural hegemony of a social group over the whole society; as the ethical content fo the state) from the sense given to it by Catholics, for whom civil society is, instead, political society or the state, as opposed to the society of the family and of the church.[16]

This and other notes from *Notebook 6*, spanning from the end of 1930 until the summer of 1931, represent the first point of arrival of a reflection that began in *Notebook 3* and *5*, but most of all in *Notebook 4*, both in the first series of "Philosophical Notes" (with particular regard to the notes on the relationships between structure and superstructure) and in the miscellaneous notes on the intellectuals (destined to converge in *Notebook 12*). In these notes, Gramsci outlined in particular the connection between hegemony and civil society, consistent in the fact that the second constitutes the privileged battleground and therefore is the exercise of the first. This connection appears implicitly starting from § 47 of *Notebook 1*, where Gramsci discusses from "Hegel's doctrine of parties and associations as the 'private' fabric of the state" that presuppose a "government by consent of the governed, but an organized consent, not the vague and generic kind which is declared at the time of elections: the state has and demands consent, but it also 'educates' this consent through political and trade-union associations which, however, are private organisms, left to the private initiative of the ruling class".[17] The link between the two concepts is made explicit in § 81 of *Notebook 6 – Hegemony (civil society) and separation of powers –* where there appears a reference to "the hegemonic apparatus" which also recalls the material character of the exercise of hegemony.

In § 52 of *Quaderno 8* ("Notebook 8", February 1932), dedicated to the *Moderno Principe* ("the Modern Prince"), recurs the expression (that constitutes a *hapax legomenon* in Gramsci's work) of "civil hegemony", presented as a composition and surmounting of the concept of "permanent revolution", that in turn is assimilated into the strategy of the war of movement, that according to Gramsci will become obsolete in the modern world, at least in the West. Vice versa, "in politics, the war of position is the concept of hegemony that can only come into existence after certain things are already in place, namely, the large popular organizations of the modern type that represent, as it were, the 'trenches' and the permanent fortifications of the war of position".[18] The military metaphor – that continuously permeates the Marxist tradition (from

---

16   PN3: 20–21 (Q 6, § 24: 703).
17   PN1: 153 (Q 1, § 47: 56),
18   PN3: 267 (Q 8, § 52: 973).

Engels to Lenin) – has the merit of underlining the conflictual character of hegemonic relations, over which Gramsci's culturalist interpretation of hegemony flies, widespread above all in the Anglo-Saxon world and based on a partial (or second hand) reading of the *Quaderni del carcere* ("Prison Notebooks"). What is more, there is still no comprehensive and complete translation of the *Quaderni del carcere* into the English language.[19] The cultural plane is actually only one of the many levels where the struggle to attain and conserve hegemony expresses itself; and this struggle does not exclude – but in fact it sometimes involves – the use of force, in a relationship that is always reciprocal and changing. Indeed, to use the same expression that Gramsci employs in § 38 of *Notebook 4* about the relationship between *civil society and political society* within a state understood in an extremely broad sense, "[this] distinction is purely methodological and not organic" because it does not find actual confirmation "in concrete historical life".[20] An example of this intertwining appears in § 83 of *Notebook 7*, December 1931, where Gramsci, speaking of "what is called 'public opinion'" (among whose "organs" he indicates newspapers, parties and Parliament), writes that this "is tightly connected to political hegemony, in other words, it is the point of contact between 'civil society' and 'political society', between consent and force",[21] thus overcoming the previous identification between hegemony and civil society. The next developments move toward a deepening of hegemony as a connecting element between civil society and political society within the state and therefore between the moment of consent and the moment of force, between ruling and dominance. Even before Marx (where the concept of hegemony does not appear *apertis verbis*), according to Gramsci, the merit of having first understood this nexus, as read in § 48 and § 86 of *Notebook 8*, February-March 1932), is attributed to Machiavelli whose book *Il Principe* ("The Prince") had been considered in the preceding § 21 as a model of a political science that was not abstractly rationalistic, but conceived as "a living book".

In § 191 of *Notebook 8*, December 1931, Gramsci posed the crucial problem, exemplified by the title of the note, *Egemonia e democrazia* ("Hegemony and Democracy"),[22] writing that

> among the many meanings of democracy, the most realistic anc concrete one, in my view, is that which can brought into relief through the

19   An exhaustive and balanced presentation of the problem is found in Pala 2014.
20   PN2: 182 (Q 4, § 38: 460).
21   PN3: 213 (Q 7, § 83: 914).
22   Cf. Vacca 2017: Chapter IV.

connection between democracy and the concept of hegemony. In the hegemonic system, there is democracy between the leading group and the groups that are led to the extent that the development of the economy and the legislation which is an expression of that development favors the molecular transition from the groups that are led to the leading group.[23]

The reflections of the following years up until the abrupt interruption because of Gramsci's failing psychological and physical conditions towards the middle of 1935, are dedicated to, on one hand, the reorganization of at least a part of the material gathered until this point (with the introduction of significant revisions, especially at the beginning) and on the other hand, the drafting of new miscellaneous notes in *Notebooks 9, 14, 15* and *17*. For what regards our specific theme, we must again examine the dynamism of the hegemony/civil society nexus in relation to, above all, a series of events that contribute to Gramsci's rethinking of the Marxist doctrine – taken from the orthodoxy of the Third International as a type of fideistic dogma – in terms of philosophy of praxis: on one hand the first signs of regression in Stalinist USSR, and on the other the strengthening of Western capitalist regimes, both of the liberal-democratic type – exemplified by Roosevelt's New Deal in the USA – and the authoritarian type – fascism elected as "Europe's ideological representation" of the "passive revolution" (*Notebook 10*, §9, April-May 1932)[24] and Hitlerism with its "manifestation of brutality and monstrous ignominy" (*Notebook 28*, § 1, first months of 1935).[25] These are all themes that require separate and individual treatment. For obvious reasons of space, we cannot dwell upon each of them here.

Bibliography

Gramsci's Works and Abbreviations

Gramsci, A. (1924), *Vladimiro Ilic Ulianof*, in "L'Ordine Nuovo", 1.

Gramsci, A. (1967), *Socialismo e fascismo. L'Ordine Nuovo 1921–22* (Torino: Einaudi).

Gramsci, A. (1971), *La costruzione del partito comunista* (Torino: Einaudi).

Gramsci, A. (2007), *Quaderni del carcere 1. Quaderni di traduzioni (1929–1932)*, Cospito, G., Francioni, G. (eds.) (Roma: Istituto dell'Enciclopedia Italiana).

NM: Caprioglio, S. (ed.) (1984), *Il nostro Marx (1918–1919)* (Torino: Einaudi).

---

23   PN3: 345 (Q 8, § 191: 1056).

24   SPN: 120 (Q 10I, § 9: 1229).

25   Q 28, § 1: 2326.

PN: Buttigieg, J.A. (ed.) (1992, 1996, 2007), *Prison Notebooks* (New York: Columbia University Press), 3 vols.

Q: Gerratana, V. (ed.) (1975), *Quaderni del carcere* (Torino: Einaudi), 4 vols.

SPN: Hoare, Q., Nowell-Smith, G. (eds.) (1971), *Selection from the Prison Notebooks* (New York: International Publishers).

SPW-1: Hoare, Q., Nowell Smith, G. (eds.) (1977), *Selections from Political Writings, 1910–1920* (London: Lawrence & Wishart; New York: International Publisher).

Other Works

Anderson, P. (2017), *The Antinomies of Antonio Gramsci* (London: Verso).

Cospito, G. (2011), *Verso l'edizione critica e integrale dei "Quaderni del carcere"*, in "Studi Storici", 4, pp. 881–904.

Cospito, G. (2016), *The Rhythm of Thought in Gramsci: A Diachronic Interpretation of Prison Notebooks* (Boston, Leiden: Brill).

Cospito, G., Frosini, F. (2017), *Introduzione*, in Gramsci, A., *Quaderni del carcere*, critical edition directed by Francioni, G., vol. 2, *Quaderni miscellanei (1929–1935)* (Roma: Istituto della Enciclopedia Italiana).

Francioni, G. (1984), *L'officina gramsciana. Ipotesi sulla struttura dei "Quaderni del carcere"* (Napoli: Bibliopolis).

Pala, M. (ed.) (2014), *Narrazioni egemoniche. Gramsci, letteratura e società civile* (Bologna: il Mulino).

Vacca, G. (2017), *Modernità alternative. Il Novecento di Antonio Gramsci* (Torino: Einaudi).

CHAPTER 11

On the Productive Use of Hegemony (Laclau, Hall, Chatterjee)

Michele Filippini

1 Gramsci Provincialized

Among the many Gramscian concepts – either coined by or substantially rede-
fined by Gramsci himself – hegemony is probably the most widespread and internationally recognized.[1] The purpose of this contribution is to demonstrate –
through three different modes of appropriation of this concept – the variety
and, above all, the political and theoretical productivity of this diffusion. The
work of the authors taken into consideration – Ernesto Laclau, Stuart Hall and
Partha Chatterjee – also demonstrates, in my opinion, a more general thesis
encompassing the entire Gramscian legacy. The thesis is the following: the
multiplication of the uses of Gramsci[2] and the plurality of interpretations
that it has generated express the specific character of its provincialization (to
use a popular expression of Dipesh Chakrabarty). But what does it mean to
provincialize Gramsci?[3] The original attempt, that of Provincializing Europe,[4]
consisted of relativizing the thought on European modernity in relation to the
plurality of political and social forms that the world had always produced. According to Chakrabarty, in order to follow this path, two classical assumptions
of modern European political thought needed to be rejected: "the first is that
the human exists in a frame of a single and secular historical time that envel-
ops other kinds of time [...]. The second [...] is that the human is ontologically
singular".[5] To provincialize – that is, pluralizing the forms of historical time
and de-substantiating concepts such as *the social* or *the political* – was, in this
case, not so much a way of rejecting Western modern thought (on which the

---

1   Given the amount of references it is impossible to present a short bibliography on the suc-
    cess of this concept. Please refer to the Gramscian bibliography online (http://bg.fondazi-
    onegramsci.org/biblio-gramsci), where one can search by theme or by the language of the
    contribution.
2   Cf. Filippini 2016.
3   Cf. Mezzadra, Capuzzo 2012.
4   Cf. Chakrabarty 2000.
5   Chakrabarty 2000: 16.

structure of Chakrabarty's book itself is based), but a way to revive it within contexts and traditions of different ways of thinking that are increasingly at the center of global processes. Chakrabarty writes:

> European thought is at once both indispensable and inadequate in helping us to think through the experiences of political modernity in non-Western nations, and provincializing Europe becomes the task of exploring how this thought – which is now everybody's heritage and which affects us all – may be renewed from and for the margins.[6]

From this perspective, the provincialization of Gramsci happened through an explosion of the use of Gramscian concepts, categories or simple terms in what we could call "global critical theory", offering proof of a substantially successful experiment. As we will see in the series of displacements of the concept of hegemony, the provincialization of Gramsci was, in fact, a harbinger of political and theoretical innovation and continues to be so today.

Before reconstructing this situation, I would like to propose an interpretation that explains why some Gramscian concepts – not only hegemony but also subaltern groups, passive revolution, historical bloc, civil society and political society, war of position and war of manoeuvre, traditional and organic intellectuals – are currently at the center of debates in several postcolonial contexts. Why Gramsci? And why now? We need to observe how these concepts are forged, or better, how they are taken from other authors and are given a new meaning in the context of the *Quaderni del carcere* ("Prison Notebooks") – to analyze the history of Italian politics. Italy (even before 1861, with the unification of all the peoples and institutions that inhabited the Italian peninsula) has always found itself in a unique position: that of being fully integrated into Western modernity – in Europe with the triumph of the bourgeoisie and the affirmation of liberal and democratic ideas – while still keeping its particular backwardness. In this place, at the same time both central and peripheral, each innovation had always presented itself as spurious, mediated and "corrupt" compared to an ideal (and idealized) model of development. This backwardness was in turn the result of an inequality paradoxically due to the earliness of some acquisitions – economic development, the history of municipalities – that eliminated the chances of a classic political development like the French or English. This delay/anticipation conditioned all of history just like the political theory of the peninsula, providing a particular field of application of concepts that are *inside* the line of modern development, but are also in some

---

6 Ibid.

way *uncentered* with respect to its principle axis. The figure of Niccolò Machiavelli for example, in being the first modern thinker in a country without any of the political conditions of modernity, represents this eccentricity well, indicated by Gramsci himself.[7]

Gramscian thought is a full-fledged part of this eccentric theoretical production. How else could we define his reflection on the peasantry – the central element of every backward country – but within the context of a West armored by the "fortresses and emplacements" of a modern civil society?[8] How could we not consider oxymoronic the concepts of passive revolution or revolution/ restoration, used to account for modern transformations but guided from above by conservative forces? And why should we try to logically compose the contradiction between the State as a "political society + civil society"[9] and the State as the sole "political society"[10] opposed to civil society, when it precisely expresses the two sides of a spurious condition that today is more globally widespread that ever?[11]

The list could continue. What interests me is to show how the Gramsci's legacy is fully part of the modern political conceptualization developed on a spurious, secondary and peripheral track, but still within European modernity, and how it lends itself in a particular mode to the appropriation of different contexts, an appropriation that never configures itself in the terms of faithful translation or emulation, but always in that of appropriation and reuse.

2   The First Displacement: Ernesto Laclau

The journey that the concept completed in this first displacement has as its starting point Gramsci's Italy of the 1930s, makes a stop at the Peronist movement in Argentina in the 1960s and 1970s, only to return to the other side of the Atlantic in the second decade of the 21st century, in particular in the countries

---

7   "It is impossible to understand Machiavelli without taking into account the fact that with
        the European (international, for his times) experience he went beyond the Italian experience; without the European experience, his 'will' would have been utopian" (PN3: 72; Q 6,
        § 86: 760). Cf. also Althusser 1999.
8   PN3: 169 (Q 7, § 16: 866). Cf. PPW: 313–337 (SP3: 243–265).
9   PN3: 75 (Q 6, § 88: 764).
10   SPN: 12 (Q 12, § 1: 1518).
11   This is one of the ambivalences that leads Perry Anderson to see Gramsci's position as
        inconsistent and incoherent; not realizing that this ambivalence is actually constitutive
        of the hegemonic reality of many social and state formations (cf. Anderson 1976). For a
        different critique of Anderson's thesis, cf. Thomas 2009: 93–95.

of southern Europe. Ernesto Laclau, the Argentine post-Marxist philosopher, is the carrier of this migration, and his development of the concept of hegemony is found in large part in the 1985 book written together with Chantalle Mouffe, *Hegemony and Socialist Strategy*.[12] Here, the emersion of the concept from the semantic field of European Marxism is read as a signal of the passing from a theory of political action characterized by economic determinism to one distinguished by political strategy based on contingency.[13] Gramsci is considered the final point of this evolution (in Marxism), which goes in the direction of abandoning the notion of historical necessity. The stages of this journey are: (*a*) Russian social democracy that opens the dislocation between actors and historical tasks because it finds itself with the task to conquer political freedom, a task that should instead be taken up by the bourgeoisie; (*b*) Lenin, with the idea of "uneven and combined development" making such a dislocation no longer temporary, as it was for social democracy, but structurally linked to imperialist politics; (*c*) and finally Gramsci, where "this hegemonic dimension was made constitutive of the subjectivity of historical actors".[14] Gramsci's hegemony thus expresses the logic of contingency in the formation of historical subjects, even if it still presents a limit:

> For Gramsci, even though the diverse social elements have a merely relational identity – achieved through articulatory practices – there must always be a *single* unifying principle in every hegemonic formation, and this can only be a fundamental class [...]. This is the inner essentialist core which continues to be present in Gramsci's thought, setting a limit to the deconstructive logic of hegemony.[15]

Laclau intends to break down this last limit, formulating a theory of hegemony that expunges every residue of necessity that is fully contingent and discursively structured.[16] Recovering the arsenal of Gramscian concepts listed above is rightfully a part of this operation which permits Laclau to recover all the richness of a Marxist theory formulated under exceptional conditions, decentralized, and thus more suited to the politics of contingent articulations. It is therefore starting from Gramsci, in *Hegemony and Socialist Strategy*, that a hegemonic-discoursive theory is constructed that will support all of Laclau's

---

12   Laclau, Mouffe 2001.
13   Cf. Laclau, Mouffe 2011: 7–91.
14   Laclau, Mouffe 2001: XII.
15   Laclau, Mouffe 2001: 69.
16   On the idea of discourse in Laclau which is specific and not limited to simple verbal acts, cf. Laclau 1990: 100–103.

subsequent works where the theme of hegemony works side by side with (partly overlying and partly substituting) the theme of populism as in *On Populist Reason*.[17] This book has had an undeniable impact in Europe, particularly on the political strategy of emerging leftist forces that are alternatives to socialist parties (Podemos in Spain, Syriza in Greece, La France Insoumise in France and also the Labour in England). The *Italian anomaly* that, reformulated *on the margins* through populist (Peronist) Argentinian categories, comes back to Europe as the ideological base of the new Left, is an explanatory image of a successful provincialization.

3   The Second Displacement: Stuart Hall

After this voyage through Italy-Argentina-Europe, let's take another direction and set a new route: from Jamaica to England. Stuart Hall was one of the prominent figures in British *cultural studies,* founder of the *New Left Review* and protagonist of the Centre for Contemporary Cultural Studies of Birmingham (CCCS). His Jamaican origins are not only a personal fact (just like Laclau is Argentinian), but are strongly linked to his studies on popular culture, race and ethnicity. Hall even uses Gramsci's concept of hegemony as a starting point for his research. In particular, such a concept is used to interpret Margaret Thatcher's construction of the conservative historical bloc in the 1980s – a bloc that was successful in appropriating several slogans that were the property of popular culture and the Left: "the process we are looking at here [Thatcherism] is very similar to that which Gramsci once described as *transformism*: the neutralization of some elements in an ideological formation and their absorption and passive appropriation into a new political configuration".[18] Thatcherism is therefore framed as a political phenomenon as much as a cultural one: "the Thatcherites know that they must 'win' in civil society as well as in the state. They understand, as the left generally does not, the consequences of the generalization of the social struggle to new arenas and the need to have a strategy for them too".[19]

The great moving right show[20] – the evocative title of a famous essay by Hall – was not chosen by chance, but was, on the contrary, conceived, constructed and put into practice as a reaction to the decay of the historical

---

17   Laclau 2005. Cf. Laclau 1990; Laclau 1996; Laclau 2014.
18   Hall 1988: 49.
19   Hall 1988: 154.
20   Hall 1979.

compromise between workers and capital, that from the 1940s in England had been tacitly accepted by all governments. Thatcherism, therefore, should not be understood as a *pathology* of the British political system, but as one of the best bets ever wagered inside of it. Not by chance, Thatcherism has a history of hard struggle within its political field, in order to impose itself on the other rightwing factions of the Conservative Party. Thatcher's masterpiece was to build an autonomous and hegemonic narration and to have understood the political nature of the cultural framework.

In this context, Hall uses the reference to Gramscian concepts like theoretical picklock – allowing him to overcome the impasse of the English "left" in the face of changes that they do not seem to fully understand. The problem of ideology returns to the centre stage of the discourse in the sense of "the languages, the concepts, categories, imagery of thought, and the systems of representation".[21] In this case, Gramsci is important because:

> he altogether refuses any idea of a pregiven unified ideological subject [...]. He recognizes the "plurality" of selves or identities of which the so-called "subject" of thought and ideas is composed. He argues that this multifaceted nature of consciousness is not an individual but a collective phenomenon.[22]

Compared to the Left, Thatcherism first understood the multifaceted and hegemonic nature of contemporary society. Against class reductionism, Gramsci thus becomes useful once again with his concepts of hegemony, historical bloc or war of position, which manage to extract from the core of Marxist thought a mediated concept of determination, not formulated in a economic manner but instead based on "relations of force".[23]

To stress once again the role played by Gramsci as a link, it is interesting to note how Laclau, coming from a Marxist background, puts himself beyond Gramsci criticizing his essentialist residuals, and how Hall, on the contrary, coming from a structuralist background, thinks of Gramsci like an embankment on the opposing front: "Gramsci is where I stopped in the headlong rush into structuralism and theoreticism. At a certain point I stumbled over Gramsci, and I said, 'Here and no further!'"[24]

---

21   Hall 1986: 29.
22   Hall 1986: 22.
23   Cf. Hall 1986: 14–15.
24   Hall 1988: 69.

4   The Third Displacement: Partha Chatterjee

The last voyage departs from the old continent bringing the concept to India, and then returns home, as is usual, enriched with the nuances and innovations that make Gramsci's provincialization a political-theoretical weapon. Partha Chatterjee, an Indian intellectual who is a member of the second generation of the *subaltern studies* group, wrote two books of interest: *Nationalist Thought and the Colonial World* and *The Politics of the Governed.*

The first book reconstructs the history of Indian nationalism by retracing three different phases. In the first phase, nationalism is the pre-conceived knowledge that colonial domination imposes on local elites. It is a "theoretical tool" that is derived from the experiences, the concepts, and the history of the colonizers. This nationalism, writes Chatterjee, is at the same time "imitative and hostile to the models it imitates".[25] This ambiguity is first cause responsible for the separation between elite and subalterns in India. It is here that the Gramscian "toolbox" comes into play:

> Gramsci's writings provide another line of enquiry which becomes useful in the understanding of such apparently deviant, but historically numerous, cases of the formation of capitalist nation-states. [...] In situations where an emergent bourgeoisie lacks the social conditions for establishing complete hegemony over the new nation, it resorts to a "passive revolution" [...] [with] a partial appropriation of the popular masses, in order first to create a state as the necessary precondition for the establishment of capitalism as the dominant mode of production.[26]

The creation of an independent state should therefore precede the building of a relationship with the subalterns. In the face of a poor organization of the popular masses during the Italian Risorgimento, Gramsci had focused his attention on the role of Piedmont: "a State replaces the local social groups in leading a struggle of renewal. It is one of the cases in which these groups have the function of 'domination' without that of 'leadership': dictatorship without hege mony"[27] (and this is the origin of Guha's *Dominance without Hegemony*[28]). The second and third phases of Indian nationalism are therefore characterized by Gandhi's activation of the popular masses and by the *passive* closing of this movement by the emerging leadership of the Indian state headed by Nehru.

---

25   Chatterjee 1986: 2.
26   Chatterjee 1986: 29–30.
27   SPN: 105–106 (Q 15, § 59: 1823).
28   Cf. Guha 1997.

Here Chatterjee suggests the parallelism with the history of the Italian Risorgimento just as Gramsci had suggested it through the concept of *passive revolution*: as Gandhi is to Mazzini and Garibaldi, so Nehru is to Cavour.

The failure to include subalterns, or more precisely, the lack of the "classical" forms of their inclusion into the national state, remains a defining characteristic of the Indian state even in its postcolonial history. *The Politics of the Governed* begins exactly from this dyscrasia between the liberal-constitutional discourse (according to which all citizens are equal bearer of rights) and the Indian reality (where these principles are actually more nuanced – they depend on the context and form an overall tenuous belonging to civil society). Through a compelling reconstruction of the political battles of the inhabitants of an informal settlement in Calcutta, Chatterjee tells us how a large sector of the population finds themselves outside of the rational and "geometrical" structure of the rule of law, but how not for this reason should its presence be considered irrelevant. The external nature of this population and the impossibility of its complete internalization make it an *internal* problem of the state. Relations that are established between state power and these "populations" are therefore of a governmental nature, based on bargaining and fighting, objectively outside the frame of liberal-democratic citizenship.

Chatterjee chooses a Gramscian concept – that of political society – to identify this place of conflict, negotiation and production of subjectivity that becomes a space of action for the subalterns. The groups that make up this political society operate through an informal yet dense network of relations often using the vote as a bargaining chip or political activism as a weapon of blackmail. Through these *instrumental uses* of the classic channels of democratic participation, the dimensions of citizenship and governmentality intersect.

What Chatterjee says concerning the concept of political society therefore is that there exists a political nature that expresses itself outside of the classical coordinates of the constitutional state and that its exponential growth represents one of the major challenges for the state. It is superfluous to note how such externality/internality and such an unrecognized but active political nature, such decomposition and pluralization of forms of citizenship, investigated in the slums of Calcutta, in reality tells us a lot about our contemporary developments in "the West".

5   Conclusion

For a partial conclusion of this brief overview of the uses of Gramsci's concept of hegemony it is perhaps appropriate to go back and ask how much this specific *provincialization* has to do with Gramsci himself: if not with his personal history then at least with the political inheritance of his legacy. On this front, there are many opinions that tend to define their eccentric uses as simple wordplay or forced interpretations. I believe instead that these *productive* readings of the concept of hegemony support at least two fundamental characteristics of Gramsci's work. On one hand, the attempt to learn conceptually and to politically propose a way out of the Marxian thesis of the increasing simplification (polarization and proletarianization) of capitalist society; on the other hand, to politically pose the problem of how one builds the strength of emancipation given the different types of work, forms of life and social identities. Tracing this type of continuity, however, also responds to another Gramscian statement: that of reconstructing a theoretical tradition of the oppressed that ensures that the "history of subaltern social groups" will no longer be "necessarily fragmented and episodic".[29]

Bibliography

Gramsci's Works and Abbreviations

PN: Buttigieg, J.A. (ed.) (1992, 1996, 2007), *Prison Notebooks* (New York: Columbia University Press), 3 vols.

PPW: Bellamy, R. (ed.) (1994), *Pre-Prison Writings* (Cambridge: Cambridge University Press).

Q: Gerratana, V. (ed.) (1975), *Quaderni del carcere* (Torino: Einaudi), 4 vols.

SPI: Spriano, P. (ed.), (1973), *Scritti politici* (Roma: Editori Riuniti), 3 vols.

SPN: Hoare, Q., Nowell-Smith, G. (eds.) (1971), *Selection from the Prison Notebooks* (New York: International Publishers).

Other Works

Althusser, L. (1999), *Machiavelli and us* (London: Verso).

Anderson, P. (1976), *The Antinomies of Antonio Gramsci*, in "New Left Review", 100, pp. 12–34.

Chakrabarty, D. (2000), *Provincializing Europe. Postcolonial Thought and Historical Difference* (Princeton: Princeton University Press).

Chatterjee, P. (1986), *Nationalist Thought and the Colonial World: A Derivative Discourse* (London: Zed Books).

Filippini, M. (2016), *Using Gramsci. A New Approach* (London: Pluto Press).

Guha, R. (1997), *Dominance without Hegemony: History and Power in Colonial India* (Cambridge, MA: Harvard University Press).

---

29   SPN: 54–55 (Q 25, § 2: 2283).

Hall, S. (1979), *The Great Moving Right Show*, in "Marxism Today", January.

Hall, S. (1986), *Gramsci's Relevance for the Study of Race and Ethnicity*, in "Journal of Communication Inquiry", 10, pp. 5–27.

Hall, S. (1986), *The Problem of Ideology: Marxism without Guarantees*, in "Journal of Communication Inquiry", 10, pp. 28–44.

Hall, S. (1988), *The Hard Road to Renewal. Thatcherism and the Crisis of the Left* (London: Verso).

Hall, S. (1988), *The Toad in the Garden: Thatcherism among the Theorists*, in Nelson, C., Grossberg, L. (eds.), *Marxism and the Interpretation of Culture* (Champaign: University of Illinois Press).

Laclau, E. (1990), *New Reflections on the Revolution of our Time* (London: Verso).

Laclau, E. (1996), *Emancipation(s)* (London: Verso).

Laclau, E. (2005), *On Populist Reason* (London: Verso).

Laclau, E. (2014), *The Rhetorical Foundations of Society* (London: Verso).

Laclau, E., Mouffe, C. [1985] (2001), *Hegemony and Socialist Strategy: Towards a Radical Democratic Politics* (London: Verso).

Mezzadra, S., Capuzzo, P. (2012), *Provincializing the Italian Reading of Gramsci*, in Bhattacharya, B., Srivastava, N. (eds.), *The Postcolonial Gramsci* (London: Routledge), pp. 34–54.

Thomas, P. (2009), *The Gramscian Moment: Philosophy, Hegemony, and Marxism* (Leiden, Boston: Brill).

PART 5

Historiography

∵

CHAPTER 12

The Influence and Legacy of Antonio Gramsci in Twentieth-Century Italy

Marzio Zanantoni

The interpretations, debates and polemics that concern the figure of Antonio Gramsci and his intellectual output in Italy (starting from his incarceration in November of 1926) have been reconstructed several times and in various ways. Throughout the succession of its various editions, Guido Liguori's *Gramsci conteso*,[1] has been and still is for all, an essential point of reference for those who want to travel through the story of the interpretations and discussions had about Gramsci over the last three decades in Italy.

I will therefore try to follow a different path, one which puts historiographical aim on the diversified influences and legacy of Gramsci in Italian culture, more than on the "dispute" between opposing and incompatible interpretations. In short, I will focus more on the conscious or unconscious use (both not so political and not only political) of the Gramscian lesson, than on the judgments (instrumental or not) of opposing factions.

Immediately after Gramsci's death on April 27th, 1937, the imminent and emerging problem in a large part of the writings, articles and testimonies that the Italian and international press dedicated to the Sardinian politician, was that of placing Gramsci in the history of Italy – within the events of the workers' movement and in political struggle. In some ways it was the moment of the first "dispute" concerning the figure of Gramsci by the differing ideologies and forces, despite them being in this moment essentially unanimous in the celebration of a "martyr" of the fascist prisons and "one of the best leaders, one of the most loyal fighters for the cause of the liberation of humanity", according to the converging words of Ercoli and Dimitrov, Nenni and Buozzi, as well as Carlo Rosselli and Camillo Berneri.

As it is noted, in Italy it was Palmiro Togliatti, the man who more than anyone else was able to claim to have shared such a closely shared path with Gramsci, who shaped the contours of Gramsci's image. For 37 years, from 1927 to 1964, through 14 writings and speeches, Togliatti gives shape to the profile, or better said, to the profiles of his friend and companion, keeping in mind that

---

1 Cf. Liguori 1996, 2012; Liguori, Meta 2005.

in each one of these texts, he was responding either implicitly or explicitly to something or someone and by doing so thus modified the features.

At the beginning of 1927, with *Antonio Gramsci, un capo della classe operaia*[2] ("Antonio Gramsci, a working-class leader"), the title would be changed to *Antonio Gramsci capo della classe operaia italiana*[3] ("Antonio Gramsci, a leader of the Italian working-class") after the death of Gramsci ten years later, and from 1949 significantly re-edited with the title *Il capo della classe operaia italiana*.[4] In those early texts, Togliatti set the profile of his party companion that would constitute the most prominent image for at least another decade. Gramsci, "the first true, complete and coherent Marxist"[5] (the implicit undervaluation of Antonio Labriola would be modified later on) in the history of the workers' movement, in the history of Italian culture and thought; Gramsci the man of the Party,[6] political militant and revolutionary organizer, "the first Italian Bolshevik",[7] Gramsci the internationalist but first of all (here introduced an essential feature of his profile), "a true son of our people".[8] In short, he was referring to Gramsci as a politician, to distinguish him – almost taking him away from the chorus, from the company – from those who in the homages and commemorations after his death, underlined the image of the intellectual, the scholar, the writer after having fought him in life.[9]

In Togliatti's first writings in the decade between 1937 and 1947, the first permanent and defining feature of Gramsci's personality and of his legacy begins to form: "Gramsci's thought in a nutshell, the most new and original aspect"[10] – his Italianness. This Italianness was a characteristic that included a collection of facets: his "proudly Sardinian" spirit,[11] his national vision of social renewal, "his socialist thought appropriate to the economic, political and social reality of our country",[12] his reflections from prison, that Togliatti begins to anticipate,[13] "the fruit of years and years of meditations and studies on fate, on the history of our country",[14] the rooting of the national and idealistic culture in the

2   Togliatti 2014a: 959.
3   Togliatti 2014a: 963.
4   Togliatti 1949: 9–71.
5   Togliatti 2014a: 967.
6   Togliatti 2014a: 968.
7   Togliatti 2014a: 990.
8   Togliatti 2014a: 991.
9   Togliatti 2014a: 967–968.
10   Togliatti 2014a: 1036.
11   Togliatti 2014a: 1034.
12   Togliatti 2014a: 1012.
13   Togliatti 2014a: 1018.
14   Togliatti 2014a: 1004.

humus (fertile ground) necessary for the overthrow of an abstract dialectic for a realistic and materialistic vision of reality, conflict and class struggle in Italy.[15] It is also relevant to note that Togliatti's preoccupation with reminding "us Communists" of Gramsci's Italianness so that "we do not believe that the patrimony of Antonio Gramsci is only ours [...] this patrimony belongs to all Sardinians, all Italians, all workers who fight for their emancipation, whether it be for their religious faith or their political beliefs [...] he thought for all of us, he spoke for all of us, he suffered for all of us".[16] Thus, Gramsci's image changes and grows over the course of one decade: it is molded with moral, intellectual and political features, whose alignments change significantly by being conditioned by two disputes – on one side with the composite constellation of socialists, liberals and catholics that thought of Gramsci increasingly as a politician and nothing more than one of the many anti-fascist intellectuals[17] and on the other side, with the resistance of the Communist world, reluctant to imagine the Sardinian thinker as a "national" man and not only as the "leader" of the international working class. What are evident here are the solicitations dictated by the current political struggle: from the initial development of a national way of constructing democracy in our country, to the need for a strategy of moral and intellectual alliances designed to give definite closure to the fascist experience. The last features that Togliatti wanted to model, have a reference from behind the scenes that was then unknown but would become public knowledge shortly thereafter: Gramsci's writings from prison. While Togliatti recalled the strong image of Gramsci's Italianness from the balcony of the Palazzo Civico of Cagliari on April 27th, 1947, in those same days bookstores were receiving printed copies of *Lettere dal carcere* ("Letters from Prison").[18] The impact of Gramsci's *Letters* is enormous and the dispute surrounding the most correct interpretation of those written and the image to offer in the form of a political and intellectual legacy in reality occurs several months earlier and in a place that was certainly not neutral: Elio Vittorini's "Il Politecnico".[19] Publishing "courtesy of the Casa Editrice Einaudi (Einaudi publishing house)", a group of 13 letters written by Gramsci at the Turi prison between 1928 and 1932 and addressed to his wife, his sister-in-law and his son Delio, Vittorini outlined explicitly in his brief introduction, in certain passages extrapolated from the

---

15   Togliatti 2014a: 1014.

16   Togliatti 2014a: 1040.

17   Cf. for example Berlinguer 1945: 27–31.

18   Cf. Mangoni 1999: 333.

19   Gramsci 1946: 5–11, with an introduction signed "E.V". Working at the Einaudi publishing house, Vittorini probably could have read the *Lettere* in its entirety and would have therefore made a selection that was not random.

context and isolated as quotations. "His Gramsci", was certainly very different than Togliatti's description. Vittorini writes, Gramsci:

> appears to us today like a man of politics that could be more sharply po-
> litical thanks to his capacity to find the cultural reasons for every issue.
> [...] He claimed the importance of the aesthetic evaluation of art along-
> side the historical evaluation, more than any other great revolutionary.
> [...] For us, in any case, in many problems the last word belongs to him,
> for the Communists and for all the Italian intellectuals.[20]

Vittorini adds a distinctive passage, causing not only tensions within the communist movement, but uses Gramsci in the same issue of the magazine in which the famous text of Togliatti is published,[21] reinforcing his struggle with the problem of the relations between politics and culture, configuring the image of the Sardinian thinker as a Marxist politician whose quality of his Marxist political being was the intellectual capacity to recognize the aesthetic autonomy of the artistic fact (art, poetry, art literature) "alongside historical evaluation". This is a use of Gramsci that will permeate the left-wing intellectual.

The debate surrounding the figure of Gramsci exploded when he was awarded the Viareggio Prize in August 1947. Meanwhile, it should be noted that Togliatti's idea of publishing the *Lettere dal carcere* ("Letters from Prison") before the *Quaderni del carcere* ("Prison Notebooks")[22] in which Gramsci's thought was most widely expressed, represented a significant anomaly in the Communist tradition.[23] In the history of the workers' movement, letter correspondence had a certain importance, but usually consisted of political and ideological letters – very rarely personal letters. Just think of the correspondence of Marx and Engels with various exponents of the German Social Democrats such as Bernstein, Bebel and Kautsky. Correspondence was essential both as a tool and as useful documents for understanding the theoretical structuring of both sender and recipient. In the case of Gramsci, the *Lettere dal carcere* ("Letters from Prison"), published before the contemporaneously written and more theoretical *Prison Notebooks*, still posed a problem for the Communist community that was negatively sensitive to intrusions of the "private" into the presentation

---

20   Gramsci 1946: 5. About this Gramscian reading of "Politecnico" cf. Liguori 2012: 81–82,
      Luperini 1971: 124–125.
21   Togliatti 1946: 3–4.
22   Cf. Daniele 2005: 76, letter from Felice Platone to Giulio Einaudi, November 4, 1946.
23   Cf. several references in Hobsbawm 1978: 367.

of a public figure of absolute moral intransigence who was also leader of the party. To the consciously defined features that Togliatti gradually outlined, the *Lettere* added another extraordinarily effective feature to the figure of Gramsci even with the possibility of a risky reception: "the world of feelings and the most fundamental affections".[24]

Here is the sentimental key that could predispose the hearts and souls of Italian intellectuals and militants alike to the reception of Gramsci not only as leader of the working class, anti-fascist intellectual, "scholar" and the "writer" but also as an intellectual and militant revolutionary whose letters reveal to all his "vast and profound humanity".[25] Togliatti's "reading" of Gramsci was so decisive that, from the reasons for the Viareggio award read by Leonida Repaci the evening of August 16th to the numerous reviews and comments that followed, it was Gramsci's humanity that was emphasized as one of his most classic traits. The Communist community and the varied constellation of Italian culture seemed to have overcome their perplexities and divergences in order to unanimously recognize the figure of the Sardinian politician as a "man, revolutionary, thinker, husband and father through and through",[26] discovering the *Lettere dal carcere* ("Letters from Prison") as a "monument of life and of indestructible moral teaching" and "Gramsci the narrator and artist as equal to the moralist, philosopher and historian".[27] As Calvino wrote: "an exemplary figure of the modern Italian" who "knew how to graft to the trunk of the most rigorously traditional Italian culture, the biting historicity of dialectic materialism".[28] Some voices were displeased, uttered with a mix of envy and political irritation[29] against that "simple follower of Croce" – as written for example by Alberto Savinio to his editor Bompiani commenting on that "almost idiotic and immoral thing" of the Viareggio Prize,[30] in relation to the dispute surrounding the Gramscian legacy to appropriate that body and mind which for ten years had suffered and worked in fascist prisons and which had written celebrated pages, such as those on Benedetto Croce. In reality, these were some of the most equivocal words, with those references (often evoked in ways that

---

24   "Avvertenza" (written by Felice Platone but not signed), in Gramsci 1947: 7.

25   in Gramsci 1947: 5.

26   Repaci in Santarelli 1991: 275.

27   Santarelli 1991: 276.

28   Calvino 1947.

29   Cf. Albertini 1947, also in Santarelli 1991: 285. For the controversy surrounding the Viareggio prize cf. Chiarotto 2011: 23–39.

30   In D'Ina, Zaccaria 2007: 508–509.

were not exact)[31] to the *Lettere dal carcere* ("Letters from Prison"), which would belong "even to one who is of another or opposing political party",[32] because, "as a thinker, Gramsci, was one of us, one of those who in the first decades of the 20th century in Italy formed a philosophical and historical mind able to deal with the problems of the present"[33] – a group in which Croce naturally included himself. In fact, Croce's review of the *Lettere* is just another opportunity to talk more about himself than about the reviewed book and to attack the most orthodox Marxist doctrine – attributed to Togliatti and the Italian Communists "armed with a philosophical catechism written by Stalin" – through the example of Gramsci and his presumed difference. Croce emphasized the Gramscian ability to interpret the specificity of literary and poetic phenomena "for their aesthetic values alone and not to love them for their ideological content"[34] – with an implicit reference to what Vittorini had observed (with quite a different intent) and the attempt to bring the Communist doctrine to the stature and tradition of the great Italian philosophers: from Bruno to Campanella to Vico. An interpretation that would soon turn out to be instrumental when shortly thereafter the first volume of the *Quaderni del carcere* ("Prison Notebooks") would be published and dedicated the philosophy of Benedetto Croce. This time, the review[35] would have another tone, when the philosopher from Abruzzo realized how much Gramsci's "philosophy of praxis" was strongly characterized by its profound critical autonomy and philosophical originality and to what heights of elaboration Gramsci had achieved while in prison. Certainly, the Viareggio Prize and the almost unanimous chorus of praise that arrived above all from the liberal and actionist area, that maybe had too conveniently interpreted "Gramsci is for all", could not help but arouse some concerns within the Communist community. Carlo Muscetta hastened to warn against Croce's subtle game of an illegitimate appropriation, almost an "ideological kidnapping" of Gramsci and to reject (with the pen of Lucio Lombardo Radice), the efforts of the "traditional culture to liquidate Gramsci by assimilation".[36]

In the context of the readings and interpretations of these months between 1947 and 1948, the position of another actionist, Luigi Russo (who was then the

---

31   Cf. for example the memorial speech given by Giorgio Napolitano to the *Camera dei Deputati* on April 27th, 2017 (Napolitano 2017).

32   Croce 1947: 86–88. Croce's review was anticipated on July 6th by four newspapers (see D'Anna 1988: 289).

33   Croce 1947: 86.

34   Croce 1947: 87.

35   Croce 1948: 78–79.

36   Cf. Ajello 1979: 109–112. For Radice's position on Gramsci cf. Ragazzini 2002: 122–155.

director of the Scuola Normale of Pisa), stands out. It was at this school (the Scuola Normale of Pisa) on April 27th, 1947, on the occasion of the 10th anniversary of Gramsci's death, as requested by Togliatti, that Russo gave an important speech taking into account not only Gramsci's recently published *Lettere dal carcere* ("Letters from Prison"), but also a manuscript copy of the *Quaderni del carcere* ("Prison Notebooks") before their publication[37] made available to him with keen foresight by Togliatti. The profile of Gramsci that Russo outlined was one that, at least in those first moments, was better able to give back to that name, to that memory, the face of a man: a complete moral and intellectual physiognomy in a sufficiently determined place in history. His profile, described with non-rhetorical[38] words, seemed like that of a rediscovered friend, but even more that of "our brother in work"[39] who from the depths of a prison "was so close to us and remembered all of our writings in a friendly way and with genuine warmth".[40] Included in that "us" were names and books that first Russo, and soon after the entire Italian culture discovered with stupefied admiration: "Croce, De Ruggiero Omodeo, Salvatorelli, Matteo Bartoli, Umberto Cosmo". They discovered the subjects that Gramsci studied in prison: from the Risorgimento to grammar; from Machiavelli to literature; from Dante to Pirandello, demonstrating a "vast culture, knowledge of foreign languages and literatures, an encyclopedic interest in literature and history, critique, linguistics and finally political thought".[41] It was as though Russo could not wait to write to Togliatti the day after the memorial at the Scuola Normale, "for me, Gramsci was a revelation".[42] But one wonders, "And Gramsci the politician?". Russo, as he himself point out to Togliatti, is "not a Communist but not anti-Communist"[43] and it is in this view that he interprets Gramsci in whose writings "after 1921 one rarely finds the words dictatorship of the proletariat, instead he talks about democratic conquest and democratic education of the proletariat".[44] In this way, where Communism appears to him like "a starting point for democratic education",[45] for the first time, Russo emphatically and decisively underlines the role of the intellectual as educator on the political path towards democracy.

---

37   Cf. Chiarotto 2011: 52–53; D'Anna 1988: 301–302; Togliatti 2014b: 95–97.
38   Russo 1947: 395–411 (later reprinted with the title *Scoperta di Antonio Gramsci*, cf. Santarelli 1991: 225–240).
39   Santarelli 1991: 228.
40   Ibid.
41   Santarelli 1991: 229.
42   Togliatti 2014b: 95.
43   Ibid.
44   Santarelli 1991: 231.
45   Togliatti 2014b: 90.

We are still in 1947, where the role of the proletariat, even from its perspective of "non-anticommunist and sincere and loyal democratic" is fundamental. Togliatti can only rejoice: the director of the Scuola Normale knew how to offer, so to speak, the "correct understanding" of Gramsci. He is no longer just a politician and scholar "impregnated with the Western spirit" and "essentially rooted in the Italian tradition",[46] but a "fighting partner" that progressive men of culture feel close to, by having indicated (as no one else did before now) the problem of the education of intellectuals as necessary allies of workers and peasants instead of lofty, unreachable teachers. Luigi Russo's interpretation of the *organic intellectual* was the most lucid and conscious, and, through decisive Gramscian guidance, undoubtedly shifted the commitment of democratic men of culture.

Russo had outlined the most empathetic image of Gramsci, one that was heartfelt and not just intellectualized by men of culture of the time. In contrast, Giacomo Debenedetti (another literary critic) developed the most innovative and penetrating reading of *Lettere dal carcere* ("Letters from Prison") that had been written up until those first months of 1947. From that moment, this reading traced a profile of Gramsci that would become indelible: the classicism of Gramsci. Debenedetti, who had personally known Gramsci in Torino in the 1920s, joined the PCI (the Italian Communist Party) in 1944 and was also a member of the jury for the Viareggio Prize. Close to the time of publication of Gramsci's *Lettere*, he wrote few dozen pages of notes that remained unedited until 1972 and were then gathered by Ottavio Cecchi with the title *Il metodo umano di Antonio Gramsci, appunti del 1947 per un saggio sulle "Lettere dal carcere"* ("The human method of Antonio Gramsci, notes from 1947 for an essay on the *Letters from Prison*")[47] as well as an article-review published on May 22nd, 1947 in the Roman edition of "l'Unità" and on June 1st, 1947 in the Milanese edition[48] with the title *Gramsci, uomo classico* (Gramsci: classical man). There is an obvious connection between the notes and the article appearing in

---

46   Santarelli 1991: 235.
47   Debenedetti 1972: 15–20.
48   Debenedetti 1947a: 3, 1947b: 3 (without the comma in the title). The two articles are also printed in Vicario 1984: 158–161 and in Santarelli 1991: 263–268, which instead includes the article from the Roman edition. For the editorial and philological details of Debenedetti's articles in "l'Unità" see Pane 2017: 1–34 (part. p. 20). In my opinion, the author erroneously maintains that the "contamination" of the parts of the two articles for "l'Unità" are derived from the "Appunti" ("notes") later reported by Ottavio Cecchi in the issue of "Rinascita" in 1972 cited above (note 47). In reality, the "Appunti" ("notes") of Debenedetti, presumably from March-April 1947, constitute the draft copy of an unfinished essay. Debenedetti then uses parts of these notes for Gramsci's "portrait" intended for "l'Unità".

the Communist newspaper. In the latter, almost all the complexity of Debene-detti's considerations and his ingenious path towards a penetrating view of Gramsci's thought disappears. Even more brilliant if we think that such a read-ing came about for Debenedetti without having the complete edition of the *Lettere* at his disposition (among these, the dramatic letter to Tania of March 6, 1933, not included in the 1947 edition) and without having read in the *Quaderni* those problematically and temporally connected "Note autobiografiche" ("au-tobiographical notes") included in *Quaderno 15* ("Notebook 15") (a text that was also excluded from the first edition of the *Quaderni del carcere*).[49] The reading of *Lettere dal carcere* ("Letters from Prison") that Debenedetti offers is in fact thought of as a kind of exploration of Gramsci's self-analysis and revolves around a conclusion that turns out to be "between the words that most fre-quently recur, [...] those of molecule, molecular".[50] Availing of the complicity of Leopardi and De Sanctis, the critic from Turin reads the *Lettere* like a "story of a soul",[51] an "autobiography of Gramsci's last ten years",[52] where plots are outlined, in the literary form of storytelling and diary – "a human method".[53] Closed in a prison cell, writes Debenedetti, conscious of his physical and psy-chological changes, time was the only direction in which Gramsci could still move. "But it is exactly that, through which man proceeds to discover and ana-lyze himself".[54] It is a procession of memories, emotions and sentiments. To arrive at an understanding of things in their "entirety" and complexity, Grams-ci carries out an analysis of time lived, memories, "sensazioni molecolari" ("molecular sensations") through that which Debenedetti identifies as "meto-do umano" ("human method"). "The human method that Gramsci proposes is nothing else but philological method, spread across the whole experience of living". It is philology applied to oneself. According to Debenedetti's reading, Gramsci seems to say, "Nothing that is human is foreign to me". This expresses "the classical ideal of man",[55] where every factor on the intimate and individual plane must be taken into account. I cannot allow myself to go on about all the

---

49   On the close link, both problematic and temporal, between the letter to Tania and the paragraph in *Quaderno 15* ("Notebook 15") cf. in particular Gerratana 1990: 189–202. Re-garding the editorial details surrounding Tania's letter and the publication of Gramsci's "Note autobiografiche" ("Autobiographical notes") and the political implications of De-benedetti's reading cf. Forenza 2013, pp. 123–136.
50   Debenedetti 1972: 16. The same theme is also taken up in the article for "l'Unità", in Santar-elli 1991: 265.
51   Santarelli 1991: 264.
52   Ibid.
53   Ibid.
54   Santarelli 1991: 265.
55   Santarelli 1991: 267.

implications of mental character linked to the theory of personality which De-benedetti reflects on in his ample notes, bringing to light with extraordinary foresight the Gramsci-Freud rapport, implications that even Gramsci consid-ers[56] and on which he himself reflects upon in several specific paragraphs in the *Quaderni* (paragraphs that not by chance will be published for the first time by Debenedetti in 1962[57]). Perhaps because it was so evocative, the Grams-cian reading of the critic from Turin was not followed up or explored after-wards. More than a decade had to pass, but Debenedetti's irreducible attention to Gramsci as "the classical man" would continue to produce unexpected re-sults in the Mondadori edition of *2000 pagine di Gramsci* ("2000 pages of Gramsci"),[58] edited by Giansiro Ferrata and Nicolò Gallo along with an under-standing with Giacomo Debenedetti and published by Mondadori, not with-out consequences on Einaudi, in the spring of 1964. Togliatti will be the one to highlight these brilliant considerations of Denendetti and this centrality of the autobiographical character of the *Quaderni del carcere* ("Prison Notebooks"), by reviewing the book *2000 pagine di Gramsci* (published by Mondadori), in a famous article in "Paese sera"[59] making scholars and militants note that out of those 2000 pages, something new was coming out of Gramsci: "something that requires a more profound reflection than that we have usually dedicated to his life".[60] It was the "person" of Antonio Gramsci that needed to be placed "in a more vivid light, transcending the historic events of our party".[61] It was the extraordinary indication of a new key to a new interpretation of an unprece-dented view of the friend and companion. From "leader of the working class" to the man who becomes a person through a "molecular transformation" that is not a simple expression of an internal drama, of his suffering as a prisoner, but "a conscious criticism of a hundred years of history in our country".[62]

If, therefore, the intellectual debate surrounding the *Lettere dal carcere* ("Letters from Prison") had first of all considered the figure, the role and the personality of Gramsci the "prisoner", it would be with the publication of the *Quaderni* that the interpretation and use of Gramscian thought would

---

56   Cf. especially the two texts already cited by Gerratana and Ragazzini.

57   Cf. Gramsci 1962. Following Gramsci's texts is *Dibattito per un'antologia di Gramsci*, in-cluding selections by Mario Alicata, Giacomo Debenedetti, Giansiro Ferrata, Franco Ferri, Niccolò Gallo, Giancarlo Vigorelli, Gramsci 1962: 14–30 (cf. in particular Forenza 2013: 131–132).

58   Gramsci 1964.

59   Togliatti 1964 (cf. it also in Togliatti 2014a: 1186–1189).

60   Togliatti 1964: 1187.

61   Togliatti 1964: 1187–1188.

62   Togliatti 1964: 1189.

intensify, developing on its three main fronts: the history of intellectuals and literary criticism, the history of Italy and the anti-Croce philosophical project.

Even in the field of philosophical studies, Togliatti's elaboration was decisive in defining the traits of Gramsci's legacy. His interpretation was focused, as it is known, on two central aspects: the affirmation of the absolute historicity of social and political reality and therefore the definition of Marxism as "absolute historicism"[63] and on the other side, the value of Italian cultural tradition, an underscoring that also involved a reflection on the relationship between Gramsci and the tradition of idealism.[64] It was Eugenio Garin who best and most profoundly delved into this work. In *Cronache di filosofia italiana* ("Chronicles of Italian Philosophy") conceived and published between 1951 and 1953 and then gathered in to a volume in 1955,[65] Garin represents a moment of rupture and contention in the historiographical debate, precisely in reference to the Gramscian lesson. The *Cronache*, conceived around the same time as the publication of the thematic edition of the *Quaderni*, had Gramsci's thought at their center, read in terms of "historicism" and "national tradition", integrating themselves in those same years with Tolgliatti's formulation. But what Garin highlighted in his research was the attempt to write, in line with Gramsci's direction, a history of Italian philosophy that was the history of Italian intellectuals – an expression of their era and not the story of a purely speculative vision of events and ideas. Following Gramsci's formula, he reconfirmed the historical task of Italian culture: the construction of Anti-Croce as a construction of another type of hegemony – a task that, in his opinion, had not yet been completed. Together with 1956 and his political-cultural reflections, even the reading of Gramsci lived through disputes and defenses. The migration of Communist intellectuals into other fields, and the modification of interpretive categories created a strong discontinuity regarding substantial aspects of "historicism" and the idea of translating Marxism into nationalist terms. In light of this, the collective editorial operation of *La città futura* ("The City of the Future"), the anthology of essays published by Feltrinelli[66] seems almost specular in comparison to Garin's *Cronache*. *La città futura* aims at a reading of Gramscian thought that is completely opposed to Togliatti's line of thought and confirms that of Eugenio Garin. In this anthology, two authors take up Gramscian thought in a philosophical scope: Mario Tronti and Emilio Agazzi, intellectuals

---

63   Togliatti 2014: 1131.
64   Cf. especially Mustè 2017: 9–29.
65   Garin 1975. In Mustè 2017 the author lingers on Garin's reading of Gramsci.
66   Caracciolo, Scalia 1959.

that were in different ways outside of and distant from the militant nature of the PCI (Italian Communist Party) and of "official Marxism".

Through Gramsci, read and used in different ways by the historicist culture prevalent in the PCI, these two presented a theoretical program having as a goal the elaboration of an Italian Marxism described as the philosophy of the praxis and scientific methodology of political action. Their principal thesis was that before the establishment of Marxism in Italy could take place, the ideology of Benedetto Croce (an anti-Marxist cultural hegemony) had to be demolished.

At the same time, such an establishment of Italian Marxism could not do without the energizing sap of the one who, towards Croce, had begun the work of demolition, that is, Antonio Gramsci and his conception of Marxism as a philosophy of praxis. The establishment of Italian Marxism during the 1960s, however, needed to demolish Croce's thought in a way that was different from Gramsci's and to liberate itself from every influence of Gentile. It could occur only through a more "genuine" re-reading of Marx's teachings. It was the consequence of this line that exactly 20 years later, another collective volume (even this an expression of a "new Left" more radically opposed to the official Left) resumed a reading of Gramsci that was in many ways analogous to the theses of *La città futura,* analogous even in the interpreters of the time, with the philosopher Emilio Agazzi who in the new anthology *Gramsci. Una eredità contrastata*, published in 1979,[67] in underlining what was "acceptable" about Gramsci's legacy, confirmed and highlighted its point of view regarding Gramsci's unfinished Anti-Croce operation and the necessity to finish it through a rethinking of Marx that was indispensable in order to overcome that "speculative residue" of Gramsci and to reconnect that "dialectical melding of theory and praxis in the structural moment of the economy that is the central point of Marxim".[68]

If, as we have previously seen, the *Cronache* of Garin constituted (in the light of a convinced adhesion to Gramcian thought) the attempt of a history of Italian intellectuals from the point of view of a history of philosophy, Alberto Asor Rosa represents, in my opinion, one who like no other, successfully attempted in the same timeframe, to write an analogous history of Italian intellectuals in the view of literary culture. While in fact maintaining some of the negative criticisms of Gramsci's thought expressed in his famous 1965 book, *Scrittori e popolo*[69] ("Writers and People"), – an illusory ideology of progress, an

---

67   Agazzi et al. 1979.
68   Agazzi et al. 1979: 60.
69   Asor Rosa 1965.

overvaluing of the intellectual function, a substantial immobility masquerading as a "philosophy of praxis", during the 1970s Asor Rosa, modifying his interpretative perspective,[70] offers with the volume *Storia d'Italia Einaudi* ("History of Italy Einaudi") dedicated to contemporary culture,[71] the most ambitious and stimulating contribution of Marxist historiography to the analysis of united Italian culture according to an original interpretation of a Gramscian model. His analysis of Italian intellectuals from the Risorgimento to the unification of Italy is also rigorously Gramscian.[72] But even before the Einaudi volume of the *Storia d'Italia* ("History of Italy"), the Gramscian model is visible in the innovative *Sintesi di storia della letteratura italiana* that Asor Rosa completes in 1972 for a scholarly work,[73] a summary in which every literary period (from the origins to the 1960s) is preceded by a paragraph specifically dedicated to *I gruppi intellettuali* ("The intellectual groups") for the first time. The volume edited by Einaudi on *Culture* thus leads to a development of the Gramscian mark on the history of intellectuals that unravels into threads and themes strongly present in Gramsci's *Quaderni del carcere* ("Prison Notebooks"). Here are a few of them: a hostility towards Leftist radicals and those democratic bourgeois intellectuals, the expression of a reforming mediation of an uncertain and abstract moral position; the attack against the abstract democratic Jacobinism and against the sectarian and masonic tradition of Italian intellectuals; the positive evaluation of Turati's democratic socialism that had permitted many young bourgeois intellectuals to view the working class as a class available to realize a program of profound moral renewal. And again: the vision of Croce as a national intellectual, creator of a high-class bourgeois operation to present as an intellectual above the political parties, according to the Gramsican reading traceable in the pages dedicated to the "southern question". The best of Gramsci's legacy in terms of the history of intellectuals appears fully deployed in the pages written by Asor Rosa: the idea of a "profound difference between the potential of culture and the real, historical world"[74] and the non-mechanical application of "the relationship between structure and superstructure that is the classical canon of all cultural histories of Marxist inspiration".[75] To me it seems like the Asor Rosa of *Storia d'Italia*, unlike the Asor Rosa of *Scrittori e popolo*, over the decades from the Risorgimento until the 1960s, develops the types of analysis and ideas that decidedly Gramscian authors such as Natalino

---

70   Cf. Liguori 2012: 240.
71   Asor Rosa 1976.
72   Cf. Diaz 1980: 181–207.
73   Asor Rosa 1972.
74   Asor Rosa 1978: 263.
75   Asor Rosa 1978: 260.

Sapegno and Giuseppe Petronio[76] had elaborated either partially or succinctly regarding the Italian literary system. In other words, Asor Rosa realized the analytical reconstruction of a Gramscian model of the history of culture and education of Italian intellectuals, in which the personality of the writer is rightfully valued and that includes, without ever isolating or over-valuing them, also literary facts and tracing them back to their historical roots.[77] This is the desired situation, expressed in the *Quaderni* ("Prison Notebooks"), of a fusion of political and ideological judgement that includes the historical reference to the object of study, and the critical judgment on the profound historical features of the literary text. In this way, literature ceases to be self-sufficient because it belongs to and is influenced by a procedural totality, which is its ideological *humus*. Against this view there is, just to mention some examples, the anti-Gramscism of Fortini or Romano Luperini, which is both focused on considering the aesthetic value as a part of political struggle and underlining the structural base of the aesthetic production, pursuing the melding of the structural method into Marxism.[78]

Another field where Gramsci's legacy was debated but also strongly valued was historical studies. In 1973, the journal "Rinascita"[79] conducted a survey of historians regarding the Marxist historical research in Italy. One of the historians interviewed, Ernesto Ragionieri, declared that, "without considering Gramsci, it is not possible to produce serious works of historical culture in Italy".[80] Such considerations of Gramsci's legacy began in the historiographical field in the middle of the 1950s, soon after the publication of the *Quaderni* ("Prison Notebooks"). From this point of view, one should not forget that the first "scientific" representation of Gramsci's prison writings that Togliatti expressed on the basis of meager indications he knew about just a few months after the death of the prisoner, was that of "a materialistic representation of the history of Italy".[81] The historian Giorgio Candeloro was one of the first to realize a similar representation in his essential *Storia dell'Italia moderna dal 1700 al 1950*,[82] published in 1956. The mention of Gramsci as the one who "had

---

76 For the "revolutionary" discovery of Gramsci by Giuseppe Petronio cf. Paladini Musitelli 2003: 76.

77 Cf. Gatto 2016: 81–83. Gatto's book constitutes one of the few recent positive additions to the field of contemporary Gramscian criticism (and not only in the literary field) noted for its wealth of analysis and information.

78 Gatto 2016: 162–164.

79 Cecchi 1974.

80 Ragionieri, in Cecchi 1974: 58.

81 Togliatti, in Daniele 2005: 17.

82 Candeloro 1956–1986.

strongly contributed to stimulating the need for re-thinking", providing "the essential lines of a new interpretation of the history of modern Italy" was made explicit from the *Preface*[83] and showed the basis of Marxist teachings: "do not stop at the cultural-political aspect of historical facts [...], to interpret the past in the light of the problems of the present and to clearly identify the positive elements, which are always a part of the system of forces and ideologies tending to stimulate the general progress of society in a concrete way and with this criteria judge men and facts".[84] Concluding exactly 30 years later, the grandiose work of Candeloro had intersected in 1976 with the other masterful work on Gramsci that provided the frame of Italian history from the unification to the end of the 1960s: the volume of Ernesto Ragionieri, has like that of Asor Rosa's, *Storia d'Italia Einaudi*[85] as its starting point. Ragionieri's work (unfortunately left unfinished because of the author's sudden death) still remains the most important analysis (in the light of Gramsci's historiographical stimuli) regarding the process of formation of the modern Italian state and its ruling class. The in-depth analysis of Gramscian themes that took place during the 1960s and 1970s developed (even with strong ideological differences) around issues that had significant political and historiographical impact. The problem of the relationship between urban and rural "reiterated with great energy in *Quaderni del carcere* ('Prison Notebooks')[86] with regards to the contemporary culture of Italy"; identifying worldwide phenomena and their specific relevance for Italy; the rapprochement to fascism as a complex and contradictory reality but certainly not a provincial one; the relationship between Europe and America in terms of the initiatives of the popular and working classes; the problem of organizing and controlling the popular masses as a determining factor the modification of the organization of capitalism, themes suggested from notes on *Americanismo e fordismo* ("Americanism and Fordism");[87] the formation of the industrial-agricultural bloc in Italy; the process of formation of our national market in relation to the specificities of capitalist accumulation in our country, problems that Gramsci described as "*central* to our Risorgimento and post-Risorgimento history".[88] The historian Emilio Sereni, in particular, delved into these themes in detail in a continuous "interview" with Gramsci, transforming into research (among the most productive of Marxist historians) the principle themes of Gramscian elaboration while seeing them without bias of potential

---

83   Cf. Candeloro 1956: 9.
84   Candeloro 1956: 10.
85   Ragionieri 1976.
86   Ragionieri, in Cecchi 1974: 62.
87   De Felice, in Cecchi 1974: 115–116.
88   Sereni 1962: 586.

or limits.[89] These limits were more strongly highlighted by those who intended to re-read Italian history from the point of view of the working class. Such was the case of historian Stefano Merli who, albeit very critical towards the tradition of Gramscian historiography, nevertheless in his introduction to his unsurpassed and weighty volume on the formation of the industrial proletariat in the last two decades of the 1800s,[90] warned against the Manichean vision of history that a working class reading produced. That type of reading that had produced its own paradigmatic text: *Proletari senza rivoluzione* ("Proletariats Without Revolution") by Renzo Del Carria, edited in 1966 and well known between 1968 and the early 1970s. Del Carria, who put a group of Gramsci's writings in the final *Bibliography*, recalled the Sardinian thinker, in a line of continuity from Marx and Lenin, as a discoverer of the study of the autonomous protest of the subaltern classes and of their becoming revolutionary classes.[91] Del Carria was the most ideologically extreme manifestation of a certain reading of Gramsci: the Gramsci who in the political battles of 1968 and in the expressions of the "new Left" of those years, became the only theorist and organizer of factory councils, the journalist of the new order, the revolutionary that changed the perspective from party to class, the theorist of hegemony of the war of position read as a search for dominion and for the violent and revolutionary act, the young Gramsci against the imprisoned Gramsci, expression of Togliatti's opportunism and of the revisionism and reformism of the PCI.

The convention in Florence in December 1977 was the last moment for a lively debate surrounding Gramsci's legacy: a debate in which the political and cultural polemics between the supporters of the PCI and its opposers found (through Gramsci and his use) the reasons for a bitter confrontation. But the convention also brought deeper theoretical and political understanding.

The last two decades of the 1900s (especially the 1980s) were the years of Gramsci's oblivion, or better, of a debate surrounding the Sardinian thinker, especially in Italy. On the one hand, they were years of expansion in the world of Gramsci's thought and on the other hand, a time of pointing out the hermeneutics as well as the terminological and conceptual clarification of Gramsci's work produced during his time in prison. This operation, which had and has in Gianni Francioni one of the most constant scholars of Gramscian philology, however, was the indispensable premise, together with the discovery and acquisition of new documentation, to add to that innovative season of Gramscian studies that had definitively overpassed – as Giuseppe Vacca wrote well,

---

89   Cf. Sereni 1962.: 599–600, Sereni 1972: 136–140.
90   Merli 1972–73.
91   Del Carria 1970: 25.

"the most serious distortion of both recent and past Gramscian studies: the dissociation of his life from his thought".[92] The two works of scholars that are decidedly different are the 2012 volume written by Vacca[93] and the new biography of Gramsci by Angelo d'Orsi:[94] the most recent expressions albeit in different languages and with different intentions.

The national edition of the writings and letters of Antonio Gramsci, now in progress, will surely offer new perspective and stimuli. It will be up to the new generations of researchers to understand how to grasp them. But this is the history of the future.

Bibliography

Gramsci's Works

Gramsci, A. (1946), *Lettere dal carcere*, in "Il Politecnico", 33–34, September–December.

Gramsci, A. (1962), *Carte inedite di Antonio Gramsci*, in "L'Europa Letteraria", II, 13–14, February–April.

Gramsci, A. (1964), *2000 pagine di Gramsci*, (Milano: Il Saggiatore).

Gramsci, A. (1947), *Lettere dal carcere* (Torino: Einaudi).

Other Works

Agazzi, E. et al. (1979), *Gramsci. Un'eredità contrastata. La nuova sinistra rilegge Gramsci* (Milano: Ed. Ottiaviano).

Ajello, N. (1979), *Intellettuali e PCI. 1944–1958* (Bari: Laterza).

Albertini, M. (1947), *Un Gramsci edificante*, in "Lo Stato moderno", 17, September 5th.

Asor Rosa, A. (1965), *Scrittori e popolo. Saggio sulla letteratura populista in Italia* (Roma: Samonà e Savelli).

Asor Rosa, A. (1976), *Storia d'Italia. Dall'Unità ad oggi*, IV/2 (Torino: Einaudi).

Asor Rosa, A. (1972), *Sintesi di storia della letteratura italiana* (Firenze: La Nuova Italia).

Asor Rosa, A. (1978), *Una risposta*, in Macry, P., Palermo, A. (eds.), *Società e cultura dell'Italia unita* (Napoli: Guida).

Berlinguer, M. (1945), in "Mercurio", 11, July, pp. 27–31.

Calvino, I. (1947), *Antonio Gramsci. Lettere dal carcere*, in "L'Amico del popolo", May 1st.

Candeloro, G. (1956–1986), *Storia dell'Italia moderna* (Milano: Feltrinelli).

Caracciolo, A., Scalia, G. (eds.) (1959), *La città futura. Saggi sulla figura e il pensiero di Antonio Gramsci* (Milano: Feltrinelli).

---

92 Vacca 2017: 4.
93 Vacca 2012.
94 d'Orsi 2017.

Cecchi, O. (ed.) (1974), *La ricerca storica marxista in Italia* (Roma: Editori Riuniti).

Chiarotto, F. (2011), *Operazione Gramsci. Alla conquista degli intellettuali nell'Italia del dopoguerra* (Milano: Mondadori).

Croce, B. (1947), *Lettere dal carcere di Antonio Gramsci*, in "Quaderni della Critica", III, 8.

Croce, B. (1948), *Il materialismo storico e la filosofia di Benedetto Croce*, in "Quaderni della Critica", IV, 10.

D'Anna, G. (1988), *La "scoperta" di Antonio Gramsci. Le "Lettere" e i "Quaderni del carcere" nel dibattito italiano 1944–1952*, in "Italia contemporanea", 211.

D'Ina, G., Zaccaria, G. (eds.) (2007), *Caro Bompiani. Lettere con l'editore* (Milano: Bompiani).

d'Orsi, A. (2017), *Gramsci. Una nuova biografia* (Milano: Feltrinelli).

Daniele, C. (ed.) (2005), *Togliatti editore di Gramsci* (Roma: Carocci).

Debenedetti, G. (1947a), *Gramsci, uomo classico*, in "l'Unità" (Roma), May 22.

Debenedetti, G. (1947b), *Gramsci uomo classico*, in "l'Unità" (Milano), June 1.

Debenedetti, G. (1972), *Il metodo umano di Antonio Gramsci. Appunti del 1947 per un saggio sulle "Lettere dal carcere"*, in "Rinascita", 39.

Del Carria, R. [1966] (1970), *Proletari senza rivoluzione. Storia delle classi subalterne italiane dal 1860 al 1950* (Milano: Oriente).

Diaz, F. (1980), *Gli intellettuali dall'Unità alla Grande Guerra*, in Tranfaglia, N. (ed.), *L'Italia unita nella storiografia del secondo dopoguerra* (Milano: Feltrinelli).

Forenza, E. (2013), *Il Gramsci "molecolare" di Giacomo Debenedetti: il problema politico dell'autobiografia*, in "Historia Magistra", 13.

Garin, E. (1975), *Cronache di filosofia italiana 1900–1943* (Roma-Bari: Laterza).

Gatto, M. (2016), *Nonostante Gramsci. Marxismo e critica letteraria nell'Italia del Novecento* (Macerata: Quodlibet).

Gerratana, V. (1990), *Unità della persona e dissoluzione del soggetto*, in Muscatello, B. (ed.), *Gramsci e il marxismo contemporaneo* (Roma: Editori Riuniti).

Hobsbawm, E.J. (1978), *La fortuna delle edizioni di Marx ed Engels*, in AA.VV. *Storia del marxismo*, 1, *Il marxismo ai tempi di Marx* (Torino: Einaudi).

Liguori, G. (1996), *Gramsci conteso. Storia di un dibattito 1922–1996* (Roma: Editori Riuniti).

Liguori, G. (2012), *Gramsci conteso. Interpretazioni, dibattiti e polemiche 1922–2012* (Roma: Editori Riuniti).

Liguori, G., Meta, C. (2005), *Gramsci. Guida alla lettura* (Milano: Unicopli).

Luperini, R. (1971), *Gli intellettuali di sinistra e l'ideologia della ricostruzione nel dopoguerra (II)*, in "Ideologie", 15.

Mangoni, L. (1999), *Pensare i libri. La casa editrice Einaudi dagli anni trenta agli anni settanta* (Torino: Bollati Boringhieri).

Merli, S. (1972–1973), *Proletariato di fabbrica e capitalismo industriale. Il caso italiano: 1880–1900*, 2 vol. (Firenze: La Nuova Italia).

Mustè, M. (2017), *La presenza di Gramsci nella storiografia filosofica e nella storia della cultura*, in "Filosofia Italiana", special issue *L'influenza di Gramsci in Italia e nel mondo*, 2.

Napolitano, G. (2017), *Memorial speech for Gramsci*, in "l'Unità", 28th April.

Paladini Musitelli, M. (2003), *Ricordo di Giuseppe Petronio*, in "Critica Marxista", 1.

Pane, A. (2017), *Debenedetti e "l'Unità": la 'Verticale' del 1946–47*, in "Prassi Ecdotiche della Modernità letteraria", 2.

Ragazzini, D. (2002), *Leonardo nella società di massa. Teoria della personalità in Gramsci* (Bergamo: Moretti Honegger).

Ragionieri, E. (1976), *La storia politica e sociale*, in *Storia d'Italia. Dall'Unità ad oggi*, IV/3 (Torino: Einaudi).

Russo, L. (1947), *Antonio Gramsci e l'educazione democratica in Italia*, in "Belfagor", 4.

Santarelli, E. (1991), *Gramsci ritrovato 1937–1947* (Catanzaro: Abramo).

Sereni, E. (1962), *Mercato nazionale e accumulazione capitalistica nell'unità italiana*, in *Problemi dell'Unità d'Italia* (Roma: Editori Riuniti).

Sereni, E. (1972), *Agricoltura e mondo rurale*, in "I caratteri originali", *Storia d'Italia*, vol. I, (Torino: Einaudi).

Togliatti, P. (1946), *Politica e cultura. Una lettera di Palmiro Togliatti*, in "Il Politecnico".

Togliatti, P. (1949), *Gramsci* (Milano: Milano-sera Editrice).

Togliatti, P. (1964), *Gramsci, un uomo*, in "Paese sera", June 19th.

Togliatti, P. (2014a), *La politica nel pensiero e nell'azione. Scritti e discorsi 1917–1964*, Ciliberto, M., Vacca, G. (eds.) (Milano: Bompiani).

Togliatti, P. (2014b), *La guerra di posizione in Italia. Epistolario 1944–1964* (Torino: Einaudi).

Vacca, G. (2012), *Vita e pensieri di Antonio Gramsci 1926–1937* (Torino: Einaudi).

Vacca, G. (2017), *Modernità alternative. Il Novecento di Antonio Gramsci* (Torino: Einaudi).

Vicario, G. (ed.) (1984), *Gli scrittori e l'Unità. Antologia di racconti 1945–1980* (Roma: l'Unità).

CHAPTER 13

The International Historiography on Gramsci in the Twenty-First Century

Davide Cadeddu

Serious attention to the thought of Antonio Gramsci was solidly established at the international level by 1977, forty years after his death. Many conferences and scientific initiatives were promoted on the occasion of this anniversary in a political context that was showing interest in the so-called "historical compromise" and "Eurocommunism".[1]

Another important reason for this growing interest in Gramsci was undoubtedly due to the publication of several anthologies in English (mainly issued in the early seventies),[2] and the work of several Latin American intellectuals who recognized a democratic version of Marxism in Gramsci's writings.[3] Later, other authors, such as Raymond Williams and Stuart Hall in Great Britain, Edward Said in the United States and Ranajit Guha in India, helped to direct attention to Gramsci's thought by drawing hermeneutical paradigms capable of explaining current events.[4]

One other factor that most certainly aided in the international dissemination of Gramsci's thought was the publication of the *Quaderni del carcere* ("Prison Notebooks") edited by Valentino Gerratana and promoted by the Istituto Gramsci (Gramsci Institute),[5] which in turn launched a new cycle of translations.[6] Today, Gramsci's writings have been translated into more than forty languages and approximately half of the literature produced yearly that is dedicated to him is written in languages other than Italian.[7]

Fascination with Gramsci grew in the aftermath of the fall of European Communism over the course of 1989–1991. At the conference "Gramsci nel

---

1   Cf. Ferri 1977; in specific, for the English context, cf. Showstack Sassoon 1980.
2   Cf. SPN, Gramsci 1973, SPW-1, SPW-2.
3   Cf, for example, Aricó 1988.
4   Cf. Williams 1980; Hall 1987, Said 1993; Guha 1983.
5   Cf. Q.
6   Cf. Gramsci 1978–1996; Gramsci 1981; Gramsci 1981–2000; Gramsci 1999–2002; Gramsci 1991–2002; Gramsci 1992–2011.
7   For the most recently updated description see *Bibliografia gramsciana*: http://bg.fondazion egramsci.org/biblio-gramsci.

mondo" ("Gramsci in the World") in 1989, the dissemination of Gramsci's thought at a global level was highlighted[8] and it was on this occasion that the constitution of the International Gramsci Society was both debated and announced. The Society held its first public meeting in New York in April of 1991.[9]

Paradoxically, Gramsci's growing international fame was countered by a progressive decline of interest in Italy where, in various ways and at various times, a reinterpretation of his thought was taken as a way to discredit both its cultural legacy and political frame of reference. Nevertheless, the international diffusion of Gramsci increased and was newly energized in 1997 (on the sixty year anniversary of his death) by the organization of two conferences promoted by the Fondazione Istituto Gramsci (Gramsci Foundation Institute) and the International Gramsci Society, both attended by scholars of many different nationalities.[10]

In 2007, a renewed interest in Gramscian studies coincided with the first volume of the "Edizione nazionale degli scritti di Antonio Gramsci" (National Edition of the Writings of Antonio Gramsci) promoted by the Gramsci Foundation Institute and published by the "Istituto della Enciclopedia Italiana" (The Institute of the Italian Encyclopedia) that provided a work plan composed of "Scritti 1910–1926" (Writings 1910–1926), "Quaderni del Carcere. 1929–1935" (Prison Notebooks. 1929–1935) and "Epistolario. 1906–1937" (Epistolary. 1906–1937).[11] A collective work of particular importance and usefulness, the *Dizionario gramsciano 1926–1937* ("Gramscian Dictionary 1926–1937")[12] was published just two years later.

There are several works that give a clear view of the situation in terms of international historiography: the series "Studi gramsciani nel mondo" (Worldwide Studies on Gramsci) directed by Giuseppe Vacca and promoted by the Fondazione Istituto Gramsci (Gramsci Foundation Institute); the republication of the volume *Gramsci conteso* ("Gramsci Contested") duly updated in 2012 by Guido Liguori; the periodical "Gramsciana. Rivista internazionale di studi su Antonio Gramsci" (Gramsciana. International Journal of Studies on Antonio Gramsci), directed by Angelo d'Orsi; the "International Gramsci Journal", directed by Derek Boothman; the *Bibliografia gramsciana* ("Gramscian Bibliography") published online by the Fondazione Gramsci onlus (Gramsci Foundation non-profit), founded by John M. Cammett and now curated by

---

8   Cf. Righi 1995.

9   Cf. Buttigieg 1992.

10   Fondazione Istituto Gramsci Onlus 1999; International Gramsci Society 1999.

11   Gramsci 2007.

12   Liguori, Voza 2009.

Francesco Giasi and Maria Luisa Righi with the collaboration of the International Gramsci Society.[13]

Once we find our bearings inside of a cultural production whose value is as vast as it is inhomogeneous, we can identify which works deserve to be included in a general historiographical analysis and which others have little to do with historiography (being more appropriately placed in the area of political and social theory or directly in the arena of political and cultural struggle with its consequent ideological uses). From the historiographical point of view, Antonio Gramsci clearly emerges as a completely complex and rare case, precisely in relation to his worldwide diffusion and to his "global" being in almost all the meanings this adjective could assume. The complexity of the situation facing us therefore suggests that we must identify some categories and, without being overwhelmed by an infinite mass of information, bring ourselves to be able to discern.

First of all, we must have a clear idea of what we mean by historiography. If everything is history, "nothing else but history",[14] certainly not everything is historiographical production, at least not in its narrow, specialized and scientific meaning. Historiographical analysis involves the historical reconstruction of past events or the historicized interpretation of an expression of human creativity, which in our case could be either political thought or the general thought of an author. The production of political theories or other various theories certainly does not belong to historiography, because they draw liberally on suggestions offered by the past, with the scope of interpreting (with some well-defined or less well-defined categories, more or less adherent to the original formulation) questions and realities that are contemporary to us or at least not contemporary to the original formulation of that thought and those categories. We were taught that historiography always springs from a present interest,[15] but must avoid the danger of falling into the temptation of allowing a commingling of past and present, with the possible consequence of an anachronistic reading of both past and present.[16]

The international fame of Antonio Gramsci, as evidenced by the production of the historiography of international relations, subaltern studies and cultural

13   Fondazione Istituto Gramsci 2007-; Liguori 2012; *Bibliografia gramsciana*: http://bg.fondazionegramsci.org/biblio-gramsci/. For the Italian context see also "BGR. Bibliografia Gramsciana Ragionata", which catalogues with concise entries all titles appearing in the Italian language (even translations from other languages) starting from 1922. At present only the first volume (1922–1965) has been published (cf. d'Orsi 2008).

14   Galasso 2000.

15   Croce 2011; en. tr. Ainslie 1960.

16   For a general view, see Iggers 2012; Galasso 2016; Iggers, Wang, Mukherjee 2017.

studies, depends on the influence of Gramscian categories, but it is completely evident that it is one thing to reason on the historiography produced around the life and intellectual output of Gramsci and quite another thing to reflect on the cultural influence that Gramsci had on the historiographical production of other areas of study. As emerged in 2007 at a conference in Rome promoted by the Fondazione Istituto Gramsci and the International Gramsci Society on "Gramsci, le culture e il mondo" (Gramsci, the cultures and the world), the main problem that needs cultural management regards the use of Gramsci (more than the interpretation of Gramsci) in subaltern studies, British cultural studies, American postcolonial studies and in the Arab world.[17]

In order to avoid making mistakes, we must therefore first distinguish, at the heart of the literature on Gramsci, at least three types of intellectual interests and, inside of these, some predominant thematic areas: (1) historiographic production and its close link with philological analysis; (2) elaboration of various formulations of social, cultural and political theory; (3) ideological usage for purposes of contingent political struggle. The most relevant thematic areas, instead, seem to be articulated according to specific focus on the categories of "civil society", "hegemony", "intellectuals", "passive revolution", "subaltern" and "philosophy of praxis", that while being of a political mold, still circulate because of their heuristic value even in other cultural areas. With this, we certainly do not want to create a measure of values (putting the historiography of political thought at the top and the other philosophical-theoretical approaches somewhere further down) but it is clear that it is one thing to reason, for example, how much of Labriola, Croce or Gentile can be found in Gramsci and it is quite another thing to reflect on his theory of intellectuals comparing it to that of Zygmunt Bauman in reference to today's society. This difference needs to be clearly present and held firm. A global author such as Antonio Gramsci, however, raises a second difficulty in the consideration of the international historiography produced around him: this exemplifies a discourse that could be interesting even for other subjects with a global profile in the upcoming years. Historiography exists regardless of the capacity that it possesses to dialogue inside of itself. The noble Italian, European and therefore Western tradition has taught us, however, that the relevant part of the pregnant significance of historiographical production engaging inside of culture, awareness and identity of a society is given exactly from its capacity to develop an intimate dialogue within itself. Now, in the case of Antonio Gramsci, we find ourselves

---

17   See Schirru 2009. For a concise view, see Vacca, Capuzzo, Schirru 2008 and Manduchi, Marchi, Vacca 2017. See also Filippini 2017.

facing two obstacles directly connected to his global being and to the effects that globalization has produced around him as a subject of study.[18]

Undoubtedly, the first obstacle impeding historiographic dialogue is of a quantitative type. Scanning the aforementioned *Bibliografia gramsciana*, one understands the material impossibility of a single human being able cope with the overflowing mass of essays and volumes published every year. This problem is certainly a characteristic of our times where with the ease of self-publishing, there is a greater certainty of making one's own writing public (at least on the web page of a private blog) and a smaller chance of actually being read. The sheer quantity of words that hit each of us every day is simply too overwhelming.

As if anything more was needed, the second obstacle, making a complete historiographical mastery of our theme impossible is of a linguistic type. As already mentioned, talking about it in positive terms, the fact that translations of Gramsci's writings exist in more than forty languages and that about half of the literature dedicated to him, produced every year, is written in languages other than Italian.[19] Clearly, this aspect also constitutes a limit to the circulation of ideas and to the complexity and completeness of the historiographical debate.

Even in recently published works by authoritative scholars, the references to studies by authors not belonging to the world of linguistics in bibliographies (or in footnotes) is relatively scarce, when compared to the richness of international production.[20] Certainly, the relevance is often connected to the place and modality of cultural expression (publishing house, journal and diffusion of the language used), but we also are well aware that this is not always the case and illuminating passages may also be found in the so-called minor scientific literature. What is beginning to be seen as true in many historiographic areas is even macroscopic in Gramsci. International historiography in the 21st century seems to be almost devoid of dialogue or, more precisely, this historiographical dialogue seems to be very limited, even despite the continuous and Promethean efforts of both the Fondazione Gramsci onlus (Gramsci Foundation

---

18   For a "more balanced history of political thought", from a global view, see Babb 2018, where the goal is "to identify the key political thinkers throughout world history", who "have had influence, substance and relevance". On this theme in general, see Middell, Hadler 2007.

19   Cf. Lussana, Pissarello 2008.

20   Cf., for instance, the recent study by Grelle (2017), which mentions only studies in English.

non-profit) and the International Gramsci Society.[21] As a historiographic subject, Antonio Gramsci has generated a phenomenology of absolute originality and relevance, exactly because of the problems that his global success poses. These problems cause us to reflect on the *ad libitum* generation of interpretations of interpretations.

The historical source and the philological attention given to the source (the original text), however, is what permits qualified historiographic production to flourish, completely mastering the linguistic data with absolute competence and sensibility, in our case written in the Italian language.[22] The fact that scholars still continue their philological excavations is therefore full of merit – producing critical editions of the *Quaderni del carcere* ("Prison Notebooks"), publishing Gramscian writings and promoting a national edition of Gramscian writings – because, as was demonstrated in the past, the renewed attention to the sources prompted new waves of interpretations of the thought and work of Antonio Gramsci.[23]

Perhaps more than in the past, alongside this renewed attention, is another concern very necessary for the purpose of feeding the historiographical debate that arises for contingent material reasons, too often left to fortuitous circumstances or to personal knowledge that one has of some authors. Certainly attention should be addressed to the problem of translation, with particular philological attention, both to Gramscian writings in other languages, as well as to the most relevant writings on Gramsci at least in Italian and English.[24] This could certainly be a privileged path for the development of dialogue and international historiographical reflection as a form of respect towards Antonio Gramsci, who, as is noted, had the most profound respect for the art of translation.[25]

---

21 See *https://www.fondazionegramsci.org* and *http://www.internationalgramscisociety.org*.

22 For example, see Thomas 2008, who won the third edition of the International Prize "Giuseppe Somani" (promoted by the Fondazione Istituto piemontese Antonio Gramsci), for the best study of Gramsci in the world between 2007–2011. For an overview of the historiographical production in Italy, see Vacca 2017: 3–19.

23 See anastatica edition of the manuscripts of the *Quaderni del carcere*, edited by Francioni (2009) and, in particular, the "Edizione nazionale degli scritti di Antonio Gramsci", promoted by the Fondazione Istituto Gramsci (2007–...). An original and philological reading of *Quaderni del carcere* was realized by Cospito (2016).

24 Cf., for example, Coutinho 1999; Italian translation 2006; English version 2013.

25 More generally, on the role of linguistics in Gramscian thought, see Carlucci 2013. On the life of Gramsci, see the biographies of Davidson [1976] (2018); Frétigné 2017; and, above all, d'Orsi 2018.

Bibliography

Gramsci's Works and Abbreviations

Gramsci, A. (1973), *Letters from Prison*, ed. by L. Lawner (New York: Harper & Row).

Gramsci, A. (2007), *Quaderni del carcere 1. Quaderni di traduzioni (1929–1932)*, Cospito, G., Francioni, G. (eds.) (Roma: Istituto dell'Enciclopedia Italiana).

Q: Gerratana, V. (ed.) (1975), *Quaderni del carcere* (Torino: Einaudi), 4 vol.

SPN: Hoare, Q., Nowell-Smith, G. (eds.) (1971), *Selection from the Prison Notebooks* (New York: International Publishers).

SPW-1: Hoare, Q., Nowell Smith, G. (eds.) (1977), *Selections from Political Writings, 1910–1920* (London: Lawrence & Wishart; New York: International Publisher).

SPW-2: Hoare, Q. (ed.) (1978), *Selections from Political Writings (1921–1926)* (New York: International Publishers; London: Lawrence and Wishart).

Translations of the Quaderni del carcere

Gramsci, A. (1978–1996), *Cahiers de prison*, Paris, R. (ed.) (Paris: Gallimard), 5 vols.

Gramsci, A. (1981), *Gokuchû nôto 1*, Guramushi, A. (ed.) (Tokyo: Ôtsuki Shoten).

Gramsci, A. (1981–2000), *Cuadernos de la carcel* (Mexico: Editiones Era – Universidad Autónoma de Puebla), 6 vols.

Gramsci, A. (1999–2002), *Cuadernos do cárcere*, Coutinho, C.N., Henriques, L.S., Nogueira, M.A. (eds.) (Rio de Janeiro: Civilização Brasileira), 6 vols.

Gramsci, A. (1991–2002), *Gefängnishefte: kritische Gesamtausgabe*, Bochmann, K., Graf, R., Haug, W.F., Jehle, P., Kuck, G. (eds.), Haug, W.F. (introduction by) (Hamburg: Argument Verlag), 10 vols.

Gramsci, A. (1992–2011), *Prison Notebooks*, Buttigieg, J.A. (ed.) (New York: Columbia University Press).

Other Works

Aricó, J. (1988), *La cola del diablo. Itinerario de Gramsci en America Latina* (Buenos Aires: Puntosur).

Babb, J. (2018), *A World History of Political Thought* (Cheltenham, UK-Northampton, USA: Edward Elgar).

Buttigieg, J.A. (1992), *Editorial*, in "International Gramsci Society Newsletter", 1, http://www.internationalgramscisociety.org/igsn/index.html.

Carlucci, A. (2013), *Gramsci and Languages. Unification, Diversity, Hegemony* (Leiden-Boston: Brill).

Cospito, G. (2016), *The Rhythm of Thought in Gramsci. A Diachronic Interpretation of Prison Notebooks* (Leiden-Boston: Brill).

Coutinho, C.N. (1999), *Gramsci: Um estudo sobre seu pensamento político* (Rio de Janeiro: Civilização Brasileira); Italian version (2006), *Il pensiero politico di Gramsci*

(Milano: Unicopli); English version (2013) *Gramsci's Political Thought* (Chicago: Haymarket Books).

Croce, B. (2011), *Teoria e storia della storiografia*, Galasso, G. (ed.) (Milano: Adelphi); en. tr. (1960) *History. Its Theory and Practice*, Ainslie, D. (ed.) (New York: Harcourt, Brace and Company).

d'Orsi, A. (ed.) (2008), *Bibliografia gramsciana ragionata 1922–1965*, vol. 1 (Roma: Viella).

d'Orsi, A. (2018), *Gramsci. Una nuova biografia. Nuova edizione rivista e accresciuta* (Milano: Feltrinelli).

Davidson, A. [1976] (2018), *Antonio Gramsci: Towards an Intellectual Biography* (Chicago: Haymarket Books).

Ferri, F. (ed.) (1977), *Politica e storia in Gramsci. Atti del Convegno internazionale di studi gramsciani. Firenze, 9–11 dicembre 1977* (Roma: Editori Riuniti-Istituto Gramsci), 2 vols.

Filippini, M. (2017), *Using Gramsci: A New Approach* (London: Pluto Press).

Fondazione Istituto Gramsci (2007-), *Studi gramsciani nel mondo*, G. Vacca (directed by) (Bologna: il Mulino).

Fondazione Istituto Gramsci Onlus (1999), *Gramsci e il Novecento* [Proceedings from the international conference, Cagliari 15–18 April 1997], Vacca, G. (ed.), Litri, M. (in collaboration with) (Roma: Carocci), 2 vols.

Frétigné, J.-Y. (2017), *Antonio Gramsci. Vivre, c'est résister* (Paris: Dunod).

Galasso, G. (2000), *Nient'altro che storia. Saggi di teoria e metodologia della storia* (Bologna: Il Mulino).

Galasso, G. (2016), *Storiografia e storici europei del Novecento* (Roma: Salerno).

Grelle, B. (2017), *Antonio Gramsci and the Question of Religion. Ideology, Ethics, and Hegemony* (London-New York: Routledge).

Guha, R. (1983), *Elementary Aspects of Peasant Insurgency in Colonial India* (Delhi: Oxford University Press).

Hall, S. (1987), *Gramsci and Us*, in "Marxism Today", pp. 16–21.

Iggers, G.G. (2012), *Historiography in the Twentieth Century. From Scientific Objectivity to the Postmodern Challenge. With a New Epilogue by the Author* (Middletown, CT: Wesleyan University Press).

Iggers, G.G., Wang, Q.E., Mukherjee, S. (2017), *A Global History of Modern Historiography. Second Edition* (London-New York, NY: Routledge).

International Gramsci Society (1999), *Gramsci da un secolo all'altro*, Baratta, G., Liguori, G. (eds.) (Roma: Editori Riuniti).

Liguori, G. (2012), *Gramsci conteso. Interpretazioni, dibattiti e polemiche. 1922–2012* (Roma: Editori Riuniti University Press).

Liguori, G., Voza, P. (eds.) (2009), *Dizionario gramsciano 1926–1937* (Roma: Carocci).

ation, in Wang, Q.E., Fillafer, F.L. (eds.), *The Many Faces of Clio. Cross-Cultural Approaches to Historiography. Essays in Honor of Georg G. Iggers* (New York-Oxford: Berghahn Books), pp. 293–306.

Righi, M.L. (1995), *Gramsci nel mondo. Atti del convegno internazionale di studi gramsciani (Formia, 25–28 ottobre 1989)* (Roma: Editori Riuniti-Fondazione Istituto Gramsci).

Said, E. (1993), *Culture and Imperialism* (New York: Knopf).

Schirru, G. (ed.) (2009), *Gramsci, le culture e il mondo* (Roma: Viella).

Showstack Sassoon, A. (1980), *The "Gramsci Boom": A Reflection on the Present Crisis?*, in "Politics & Power", 1, pp. 203–211.

Thomas, P.D. (2008), *The Gramscian Moment: Philosophy, Hegemony and Marxism* (Leiden: Brill).

Vacca, G. (2017), *Introduzione. Gli studi gramsciani oggi in Italia*, in Vacca, G., *Modernità alternative. Il Novecento di Antonio Gramsci* (Torino: Einaudi, 2017).

Vacca, G., Capuzzo, P., Schirru, G. (eds.) (2008), *Studi gramsciani nel mondo. Gli studi culturali* (Bologna: il Mulino).

Williams, R. (1980), *Problems in Materialism and Culture: Selected Essays* (London: Verso).

Bibliographic Abbreviations

AGR: Forgacs, D. (ed.) (2000), *The Gramsci Reader. Selected Writings 1916–1935* (New York: NYU Press).

CW: Forgacs, D., Nowell-Smith, G. (eds.) (1985), *Selections from Cultural Writings* (Cambridge, MA: Harvard University Press).

FSPN: Boothman, D. (ed.) (1995), *Further Selections from the Prison Notebooks* (Minneapolis: Minnesota University Press).

HPC: Cavalcanti, P., Piccone, P. (eds.) (1975), *History, Philosophy and Culture in the Young Gramsci* (St. Louis: Telos Press).

LC: Caprioglio, S., Fubini, E. (eds.) (1965), *Lettere dal carcere* (Torino: Einaudi).

LC2: Santucci, A. (ed.) (1996), *Lettere dal carcere. 1926–1937* (Palermo: Sellerio).

LT: Natoli, A., Daniele, C. (eds.) (1997), A. Gramsci, T. Schucht, *Lettere. 1926–1935* (Torino: Einaudi).

NM: Capioglio, S. (ed.) (1984), *Il nostro Marx (1918–1919)* (Torino: Einaudi).

PN: Buttigieg, J.A. (ed.) (1992, 1996, 2007), *Prison Notebooks* (New York: Columbia University Press), 3 vols.

PPW: Bellamy, R. (ed.) (1994), *Pre-Prison Writings* (Cambridge: Cambridge University Press).

Q: Gerratana, V. (ed.) (1975), *Quaderni del carcere* (Torino: Einaudi), 4 vols.

SPI: Spriano, P. (ed.), (1973), *Scritti politici* (Roma: Editori Riuniti), 3 vols.

SPN: Hoare, Q., Nowell-Smith, G. (eds.) (1971), *Selection from the Prison Notebooks* (New York: International Publishers).

SPW-1: Hoare, Q., Nowell Smith, G. (eds.) (1977), *Selections from Political Writings, 1910–1920* (London: Lawrence & Wishart; New York: International Publisher).

SPW-2: Hoare, Q. (ed.) (1978), *Selections from Political Writings (1921–1926)* (New York: International Publishers; London: Lawrence and Wishart).

Index

www.Ingramcontent.com/pod-product-compliance
Lightning Source LLC
Chambersburg PA
CBHW070932030426
42336CB00014BA/2644